The
Marketing
Edge

The Marketing Edge

The New Leadership Role of Sales & Marketing in Manufacturing

George E. Palmatier
and
Joseph S. Shull

John Wiley & Sons, Inc.
New York · Chichester · Brisbane · Toronto · Singapore

Contents

Acknowledgments

Just as running a successful manufacturing company requires a team effort, writing a book about a new subject often needs the thoughts, energies, and support of colleagues, friends, and family. This book is no exception. First and foremost, we owe our deepest appreciation to our friend and teacher Dick Ling for sharing his insights relative to demand management with us. We also thank Walt Goddard and Peter Skurla for helping to sharpen our focus in the following pages.

Hats off to Dana Scannell for believing in our work and coordinating this book project, and to his colleagues and staff at the Oliver Wight Companies for supporting our work on the manuscript and helping to bring it to fruition. Thanks, too, go to Steve Bennett and Coco Crum, professional business and technical writers, who helped us organize our ideas and translate words into print.

Additional thanks go to Jim Prevatte, Joe Deck, and Steven Riggs for their efforts in helping us bring the book to its final draft. And we must acknowledge the work of Norm Scott whose cartoons provide us with some humor.

Lastly—but most importantly—we deeply thank our wives, Nadine Palmatier and Jodie Shull, for waiting patiently while we clicked away at our word processors throughout the winter nights. We'd like to acknowledge especially our debt to Jodie, for the many hours she spent editing early drafts of the manuscript, bringing her keen knowledge of English to bear. Without her help, we would still be fumbling with the introduction.

Foreword

Richard C. Ling
President, Richard C. Ling, Inc.

As George and Joe endeavored to finish *The Marketing Edge,* I was thickly in the midst of co-authoring *Orchestrating Success*, a book on the Sales and Operations Planning process. One of my clients asked me why we needed a whole book on marketing and why *The Marketing Edge* shouldn't be included as a chapter in my own book. "After all," he said, "once you explain to marketing how to prepare a forecast and tell sales how to put together a sales plan, what more needs to be said? Isn't the real action with MRP II at the production end?"

That was a very telling question, as it bespeaks an imbalance in our philosophy of manufacturing. For the past twenty years, we've been preoccupied with production scheduling and material requirements planning, often ignoring the vital role that sales and marketing play in assuring that a company is actually manufacturing products that our customers want. In fact, we used to call the aggregate planning process of Sales and Operations Planning "production planning."

Today, things are different. We have begun to realize that *demand* is what drives MRP II, and that a company's sales force and marketing arm are integral components of the demand management process. If you are part of a sales or marketing department, you can take heart in the fact that your story is about to be told. Here is a book that validates the important leadership role that you and your colleagues can and must take in assessing and communicating demand. It carefully explains the contributions you can make in order to provide the level of customer service that you seek.

Just as important, it tells you the pitfalls that can spoil your efforts. Based on my years of consulting and teaching courses for the Oliver Wight Education Associates, I can truly say this is a book long overdue. And it's certainly fitting that George Palmatier and Joe Shull should be the ones to write it. Seven years ago, they wrote a ground-breaking article on how sales and marketing can use manufacturing as a competitive weapon. Today, they bring you a comprehensive work that can improve dramatically the way your company performs in the marketplace.

Competing in the Global Marketplace

Winners got scars, too.
—Johnny Cash

END OF AN ERA

The world of the manufacturing company has changed significantly over the past two decades. Customers' expectations regarding quality, reliability, price, and on-time delivery performance have been increasing continually. Global competition, changing technologies, shorter product life cycles, and greater and more frequent changes in every aspect of the business have become the norm. As a consequence, the need for companies to utilize their manufacturing resources more wisely and more effectively has become widely accepted. Significant advances toward this end have been made in the manufacturing profession, though we are still only scratching the surface compared with what can be done.

A tremendous amount has been written suggesting ways for manufacturing companies to become more productive, and help is readily available for manufacturing professionals to learn the manufacturing philosophies, methods, and techniques that are proving necessary to compete. Quality in all aspects of a business, effective planning and scheduling systems, the continuous and relentless elimination of waste, and the flexibility to change are clearly recognized as keys to competitive survival.

In the past two decades, we have seen the evolution of Manufacturing Resource Planning (MRP II), Just-in-Time (JIT), and total quality control (TQC) as tools for manufacturing departments to improve their companies' competitive position. Comparatively little change has occurred, however, in truly integrating manufacturing with the demand side of the business with sales and marketing. The tools are there to accomplish this integration, and while many companies are doing it well, most companies are still operating with rigid departmentalization and its incumbent problems. In the next decade, we will undoubtedly see the need for major improvements in this area for a company to succeed, perhaps just to survive.

It is unfortunate that most companies do not initiate change simply to improve, but are usually spurred on by pain. The companies referred to most in literature as achieving manufacturing excellence are those companies that had to take action simply to survive. But why not take the initiative to improve in order to stay ahead of the competition rather than to just catch up or hang on? We hope this book will stimulate sales and marketing professionals, along with manufacturing professionals, to work together to begin this improvement process in their companies.

Improved performance in all areas of the company is possible when a team approach is used in running the business. We believe that the time is now for sales and marketing to lead the effort in becoming more competitive in the global marketplace.

UNITED WE STAND, DIVIDED WE FALL

In this new era of increased competition, life in a manufacturing company is no longer simple. It used to be the engineering organization designed products, the factory made the products that engineering designed, marketing promoted the products that the factory made, and sales sold the products that marketing promoted. Division of labor at its best? Not today.

The premise of this book is that labor must be united, rather than divided for companies to gain a marketing edge on today's marketplace. Consider this fact: quality experts claim that 20 percent of a product's quality defects occur on the production line; 80 percent occur during the other phases of developing, selling, and producing a product.[1] Yet, the manufacturing department, rather than the other functions and departments in a company, has been the central focal point for improving quality and productivity. Out of these efforts to improve have evolved systems and technologies, like MRP II, JIT, and TQC.

These same tools can be employed by sales and marketing to help determine how a company can best utilize its manufacturing resource. By using these tools, sales and marketing can work cooperatively with manufacturing to determine what should be manufactured, with what priority, in order to best satisfy customers' requirements. All too often, these decisions are left up to the manufacturing department's best guesses.

We believe sales and marketing must become more involved in helping a company manage demand in determining how to utilize its manufacturing resource because:

1. Customers don't buy according to manufacturing's best guesses, and
2. sales and marketing are close to the customers and, therefore, have the best knowledge of their customers' intentions.

In companies where sales and marketing are not actively involved in working with manufacturing to manage demand, adversarial relationships between the departments are common. A typical complaint of salespeople is that manufacturing cannot deliver a product on time. A common complaint by manufacturing people is that sales will not sell what has been produced.

We know firsthand that the division between manufacturing and sales and marketing can be overcome when sales and marketing take the lead in actively managing demand. We have experienced the beneficial effects on overall company performance when sales and marketing take a leadership role in resource planning.

We also know that this leadership role in managing demand can cause sales and marketing people to become uncomfortable. How do we know? We've been there. And when it was first pointed out to us

1. "The Push for Quality," *Business Week*, June 8, 1987.

that we were not doing our jobs satisfactorily and were contributing negatively to the company's performance by not leading the demand management process, we weren't just uncomfortable, we were downright defensive.

LESSONS FROM THE BATTLEFIELD

The Marketing Edge is derived from our years as managers in sales and manufacturing organizations and from consulting for various manufacturing companies. We've worked with companies that have formal Manufacturing Resource Planning systems, as well as those that still connect with the marketplace by the seats of their pants. The difference between the two is so great, the ability to direct and control the business is so tremendous, that we felt compelled to write down our thoughts and share them with others who are striving to help their companies achieve topflight performance.

Our views are particularly influenced and shaped by our common experience at Bently Nevada Corporation, a manufacturer of electronic instruments used to monitor rotating machinery. Bently Nevada is a pioneer in the development and implementation of MRP II as well as a Class A manufacturer (see appendix A for requirements for attaining Class A MRP II status). To explain our point of view, we'd like to digress a moment and tell you the Bently Nevada story. It illustrates the kind of journey you may embark upon when you integrate active demand management with MRP II in your company.

Before Bently Nevada brought MRP II on line, promises for customer deliveries were based on best guesses made "from the hip." Often, the actual shipment results were twice the promised delivery lead time, and the sales force expended a lot of energy chasing customer orders through the factory. This created fierce antagonism between the various organizations within the company, which in turn made Bently Nevada a less than pleasant place to work for many employees.

Then a fortuitous disaster struck: one of the two key manufacturing sites had a fire. We say "fortuitous" because the incident forced the company to rethink its entire manufacturing planning process. First of all, before the fire, we were a highly self-sufficient, vertically integrated company. We made our own sheet metal parts, printed circuit boards, and so forth, all via an order-point, shortage-expedite production planning system. Prior to the fire, the problems in our planning system remained hidden because we could always ram an order out the door, though often at a significant cost. After the fire, we had to purchase a great deal of materials and subcomponents from outside vendors who couldn't allow themselves to be treated as unprofessionally as we had been treating ourselves.

The company tried all the traditional production and inventory control approaches, coupled with hiring additional people and increasing inventory levels to overcome the customer delivery problems caused by the fire. Customer service continued to decline, however, and cash drains caused by higher costs and poor shipment performance continued. At that time, the president and owner, Donald E. Bently, realized that the very life of the company was at stake. After listening to the late Oliver Wight lecture at a conference sponsored by IBM, he concluded that the company desperately needed a formal planning system, Material Requirements Planning, which later evolved into Manufacturing Resource Planning, MRP II. To deal with the problem, Bently quickly assembled an MRP project team, which included members from various departments within the company. Within months, a hardware and software system had been selected, and shortly after that, the initial MRP implementation was under way.

Following initial implementation, customer service showed dramatic improvements as the formalized production planning system began ordering matched sets of parts. Parts shortages decreased, and the enhanced visibility afforded by the system allowed people to start working through potential problems in advance, rather than after delivery problems had occurred. Before the implementation of MRP, life at Bently Nevada was like reliving the Civil War, department fighting department, colleague against colleague. With the early system, we experienced a semblance of teamwork that appeared to be taking us in a positive direction.

Although our initial system reduced the immediate problems by giving production and inventory control better visibility and a better tool to plan manufacturing, sales and marketing took a back seat, rather than a lead role, in the process. Delivery lead times stretched out and inventory rose. Soon, everyone began hedging on forecasts and production schedules, which led to an "overloaded master schedule"—a condition in which more business is scheduled than can be built. When the master schedule is overloaded, the delivery dates in the system become inaccurate and all of the problems of an informal control system resurface. This ultimately causes the priority system on the shop floor to break down, and the company then operates in the same old way even though it has implemented MRP. As a result of our master schedule problem, the bloom of the new system was short-lived.

It was during the midst of these problems that Donald Bently gave sales and marketing a mandate to improve their level of participation in the manufacturing system. Since we were naturally responsive to the owner's suggestion, we both became committed more strongly to the MRP planning process. As a result, Bently Nevada entered the next phase in its evolutionary MRP II journey, which entailed putting a demand management system in place. This began with our making more aggressive efforts at forecasting and learning how to do master production scheduling, and later by our learning about Sales and Operations Planning.

Why did we wait so long to do something as obvious as Sales and Operations Planning? The MRP educators and consultants had emphasized that Sales and Operations Planning really drives an MRP II system, but it just didn't seem as "sexy" as Capacity Requirements Planning or other manufacturing techniques, which we knew had to be included in the system. Perhaps of more significance was the fact that the MRP project had been "manufacturing driven." People in sales and marketing had participated passively in the process, rather than leading it actively and aggressively.

Not surprisingly, it took us six weeks to put in a bare-bones "production planning system," and when we sat down to have our first Sales and Operations Planning meeting, it took us a day and a half to reach a consensus on the company plan. But to our surprise, we also saw nearly instantaneous results. That spurred us on, and within five months we became fairly proficient at the process. The marathon meetings shrank from twelve hours a month to one or two hours. Our customer service began improving rapidly, and profits rose to an all time high.

End of story? No. The acid test came during the recession of 1981–82. Much of our business was tied to oil, since our principal product line was used to monitor high speed refining and pumping equipment. Unfortunately for us, during this period, oil companies slashed their capital budgets. But despite the turndown, because of our Sales and Operations Planning process coupled with MRP, we had control of the business and were able to manage the company effectively even during the downturn. We were still able to maintain profit levels while many of our competitors swam in a sea of red ink, forcing them to cut expenditures on key projects that were necessary for them to maintain market share.

WHO SHOULD READ THIS BOOK

In this book, we relate our experiences as well as the experiences of other companies in developing and implementing a process, led by sales and marketing, for actively managing demand, or demand management. This book isn't written just for sales and marketing people, however. It's also written for manufacturing and corporate management who strive to form a cooperative team effort in better utilizing their company's resources.

Naturally, there is a lot of mistrust at first. But as we will show, product availability and lead times become competitive weapons instead of millstones when sales and marketing utilize the MRP II tool to actively manage demand. And the qulaity of life for sales and marketing people as well as those in manufacturing can improve dramatically. When sales and marketing communicate to manufacturing detailed information on anticipated demand that can be used to manage manufacturing resources more reliably and establish production priorities, a relationship based on trust is developed and maintained. Manufacturing people can concentrate their efforts on improving product quality and production efficiency, rather than coping with the crisis of past-due orders. Equally important, the sales force can spend its time dealing with customers and developing new business rather than fighting with the factory to expedite orders. And, most important of all, when a company delivers as promised, that gains satisfied, long-term customers.

In this book, we'll take you through the process of developing trust and honesty between departments and with customers through active demand management. The first chapter explores the deep-seated nature of problems many manufacturing companies experience today and provides an understanding of how faulty communication can diminish customer service and consume valuable resources. The second chapter discusses the leadership role that sales and marketing should play in developing marketing/manufacturing strategies. Chapters 3 through 5 cover demand planning, including forecasting, sales planning, and Sales and Operations Planning. The sixth and seventh chapters explain how to turn plans into reality through master production scheduling and how to reduce the uncertainty of demand through demand stream analysis and demand management. Chapter 8 presents an approach to getting started in improving your overall company performance.

We believe that our experiences and our mistakes can help guide you to your goals, and help you avoid making costly errors. At the same time, it would be naïve for us to expect that a single book will provide all that is necessary for a manufacturing company to embrace a new business philosophy. But we also know that it takes only a spark to fire up the engines of change. If we can ignite that spark at your company, then we will consider our efforts to be a great success.

George E. Palmatier
Minden, Nevada

Joseph S. Shull
San Diego, California

The
Marketing
Edge

Chapter 1

Reach for the Sky!

Wars may be fought with weapons, but they are won by men.
—**George S. Patton**

LEVELS OF PAIN

In the introduction, we mentioned that change in the way companies operate their business is often precipitated by reaching a high level of pain. That pain is most often caused by a decline in revenues and/or profits, a loss of market share, or the recognition of a life-threatening competitor. Too often, however, companies are surprised by this sudden pain.

When the situation is finally examined, usually it's clear that there have been warning signals all along, signals that have been ignored. The deterioration of company performance can be likened to a man who suffers from coronary heart disease; his lab tests show he has high cholesterol levels, but he doesn't think about changing his diet until he feels the searing pain in his chest.

Companies tend to ignore warning signals, too, because they still feel healthy as evidenced by growth in sales and acceptable profit levels. But, in truth, they're often vulnerable. All it takes is one significant competitor to outperform them, and the pain threshold has been reached.

What is your company's pain level? Are you experiencing any of the following common warning signals?

- You seldom meet the first promised delivery date to customers.
- Your product availability and delivery lead times are behind the competition's.
- You have little or no available information for establishing realistic delivery dates.
- Consistently poor product quality requires repairs either by your field support personnel or factory.
- A major portion of every day is spent expediting orders.
- Your total product cost in terms of material, labor, and overhead is high.
- Your dollar investment in inventory, components, work in process, and finished goods is high.
- Your inventory records are inaccurate.
- The financial figures provided through corporate planning are ignored; each department in your company keeps its own set of figures.
- Financial goals consistently are not met.
- Financial surprises pop up at the end of accounting periods.

If your company is encountering any of these typical problems, it may be indicative that it's headed on a downward spiral and change is in order. In this chapter, we'll explore how these problems can set a company on a downward spiral leading to loss of market share and financial instability. Then we'll reverse the spiral and see how the various organizations within a company can augment each other for optimal customer service and improved financial performance.

SPIRALS OF DOOM

In the Midst of Cannibals

Traditionally, the sales and marketing organizations have been responsible for bringing home the bacon—attracting business and booking orders. They have had little direct responsibility for working with the manufacturing organization in determining the quantities and priorities of products to be built. Instead, the responsibility has fallen almost entirely upon the company's production and inventory control departments, which report to the manufacturing department.

When manufacturing is left to determine what items the company will make without specific direction from sales and marketing, product availability and lead times are often unacceptable. Although manufacturing is often blamed for poor product availability and long lead times, it isn't necessarily at fault. When manufacturing does not receive detailed formal input from sales and marketing on when specific products are expected to be ordered and when customer delivery is required, manufacturing personnel can only guess at what products will be needed, based on historical data—it's not within the scope of their job to monitor the company's customer needs.

Yet, customers are constantly changing preferences as goods go in and out of vogue and the march of science and technology creates new demands and markets. That means, without clear market visibility, the company probably won't have the right product mix available at the right time. Equally likely, with an informal production planning system, it won't have the right combination of materials to finish a particular product to meet a promised delivery date. Often, numerous partially completed orders sit at the shipping dock collecting dust. The company may even have to "cannibalize" one product, stripping some of its parts, to complete an order for another customer. In a recent conversation with a manufacturing manager in the Midwest, we learned that as many as 70 percent of his company's finished products were being cannibalized to make customer shipments! The result: longer and longer product lead times, higher costs, poorer quality, and dissatisfied customers.

The Quick Fix: Up the Ante

As customer service gets worse, management's typical knee jerk response is to increase capacity and inventory. A logical solution? Sure. But it's often the wrong solution—manufacturing is still operating in a vacuum, basing its production decisions largely on historical knowledge and rough growth objectives. Customer demand may still be out of sync with the products in the company's inventory and on the production line. Further, increasing inventory merely ties up materials, capacity, and cash that could be used to promote existing products and develop new ones, both of which are necessary to the health and vitality of the company.

For example, we're familiar with an electronics enclosure supplier[1] who was unable to provide adequate customer service since they were not delivering orders to customers on time. As a result, the management decided to increase capacity by purchasing a new mill to fabricate components for a certain product, which we'll call Product A. Manufacturing purchased the mill, anticipating growth in demand for Product A. Customer demand, however, was switching from Product A to Product B, which manufacturing could have handled if a formal method of communicating changes in anticipated demand had been in place. Salespeople had discussed the product mix changes with their managers, but the information was not passed along to those in manufacturing who needed the information to respond to the product mix changes. The new mill, unfortunately, was not large enough to fabricate components for the B product line. Consequently, the company's original problem worsened; it now had excess capacity for Product A, valuable cash tied up in the Product A mill, and still lacked capacity to make Product B. Since the bulk of the demand was for Product B, customer service continued to decline.

Take a Number, Get in Line

Further slipping down the spiral, the sales force begins expediting orders in response to impatient customers. Of course, the plant can rush only so many orders at once, so expediting tends to operate on the squeaky-wheel principle: whoever squeaks the loudest gets the shipment. As one order gets rammed through the pipeline, others lag behind.

For example, after the fire at Bently Nevada, there were numerous late orders on the books and numerous customers calling to expedite

---

[1] Case studies and examples in the following pages are based on incidents at actual companies. In most examples, the names of the companies have been deleted, and in some instances the exact circumstances of an incident have been modified slightly to protect confidentiality.

their orders. The official priority system gave preference to whoever called last and to whom they spoke. For example, if customers spoke to Don Bently, the owner of the company, their orders were the next to go out the door.

Expediting also has the nasty effect of dramatically increasing the cost of product. First, if raw materials or components have to be ordered on an emergency basis without providing vendors with sufficient lead time, the company won't be able to take advantage of quantity or special discounts. As a result, it will pay top dollar for parts, components, and other raw materials. Also, when the company has to produce orders on a rush or emergency basis, it will likely pay premium shipping charges. In addition, manufacturing will often be forced to break into machine setups, resulting in extra costs and a reduction of output. Finally, overtime wages may have to be paid to complete the order.

The net result of expediting? Shortages, stock outs, missed delivery dates, and higher costs that translate into dissatisfied customers, customers who may well look to suppliers who are more responsive and competitive. Finally, expediting means that the sales force has to spend more time making excuses than booking orders, challenging the rationale for the company's very existence.

The Divided Company

As the pressure to satisfy customers builds, and the increased costs cause a push for higher prices, so does the frustration level within the company. This is often vented by unproductive finger-pointing and destructive competition for internal resources. Sales and marketing claim that manufacturing can't live up to its end of the bargain, and manufacturing believes that sales and marketing make unreasonable demands. We often hear sales and marketing people say, "Manufacturing can't produce. They miss all of their due dates. They simply can't be trusted." Simultaneously, we hear manufacturing people say, "Sales and marketing have no idea about what it takes to manufacture a product. They keep making promises to customers that we can't possibly meet. It's no wonder we have unhappy customers."

Within this environment, any semblance of teamwork is gone, and the situation can reach crisis proportions as stock outs occur, lead times become even longer, more promised order dates are missed, and new product introductions are delayed. In short, the company's ability to compete becomes jeopardized. At that point we sometimes see new management knocking on the front door (see figure 1.1)

Does this scenario sound extreme? Just pick up the *Wall Street Journal* or *Business Week* and read the accounts of troubled manufacturing companies. The downward spiral might continue for years before action is taken, and some companies might find themselves in an ''arrested state of development'' in which they've stemmed the decline, but they aren't making any progress either. They simply struggle along until a competitor decides to do the job better.

This is not to say that demand being out of sync with manufacturing capabilities is the only reason companies stagnate. While a resource planning system that provides quality company communications is a prerequisite for long-term success, it will not make up for deficiencies in product design, market coverage, and/or poor product quality. But, no company *has* to be headed for trouble because of a lack of communication between its internal organizations. By employing a resource planning system with active demand management to foster teamwork, customer demand can be matched with manufacturing capabilities to turn the downward spiral upward.

REVERSING THE SPIRAL

Companies that want to operate on a high performance, upward spiral must have a Manufacturing Resource Planning (MRP II) system in place; it is nearly impossible to continue to run a company at peak performance without an effective business control system. The annals of business history are filled with entries about companies that reaped benefits from MRP II far beyond their wildest expectations. One manufacturer of metal fencing actually used MRP II to grow and prosper during an industry downturn. In fact, this company not only held its own, but also walked off with a chunk of the competition's market share. Why? Because MRP II allowed it to quickly synchronize its

Figure 1.1

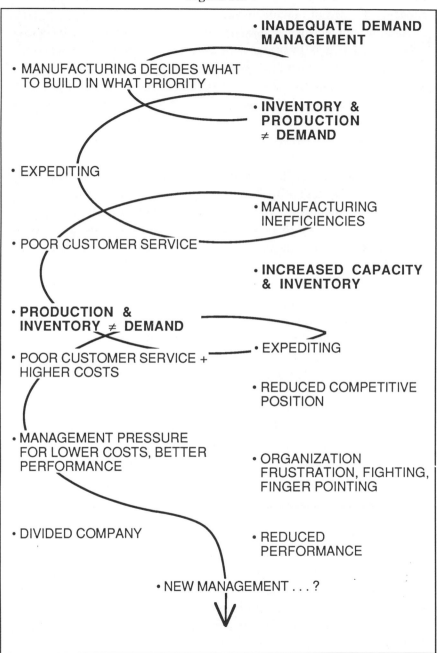

The downward spiral, resulting from customer demand being out of sync with manufacturing capabilities.

production with the needs of its customers and remain profitable by reducing the cost of manufacturing.

As powerful as MRP II may be, though, most companies have discovered that if it is to bring manufacturing activities in closer touch with customer needs and ordering patterns, the front-end input for the system must be current information on anticipated demand. There's an old saying, ''Garbage in, garbage out.'' When a planning system relies only on history, rather than current information on anticipated customer needs, the system will provide little usable information to its users.

The upward spiral, then, begins with active demand management (see figure 1.2), which involves constant monitoring and frequent review and communication of changes that are occurring in the market. This is what is meant when we use the term *driven by demand*. With demand management in place, changes in the marketplace are communicated formally to the company at both the aggregate and detail level. When we use the terms *aggregate* and *detail level* in this book, aggregate means product groupings or families. Detail level means the breakdown, or mix, of products within product groupings or families.

As we move up the spiral, the forecasts and plans from sales and marketing are frequently and formally communicated to manufacturing, so that manufacturing can generate better production schedules. Moreover, because of its Manufacturing Resource Planning tools, the company schedules production so that its parts and finished goods inventory are maintained at appropriate levels, providing excellent customer service while minimizing added inventory costs. Shortages and expediting are minimized, thereby reducing costs and improving manufacturing performance to plan. Availability and lead times are also within chosen limits, and promised ship dates can be met.

At this point in the spiral, management has gained better control over the manufacturing operation. This helps reduce costs, since unnecessary overtime and excess inventory and capacity will be cut, and leads to more competitive pricing, better margins, or both, as inefficient expediting and its attendant costs will have been minimized. Better pricing, coupled with better product availability, results in an improved competitive position, which naturally results in an improved financial position.

Figure 1.2

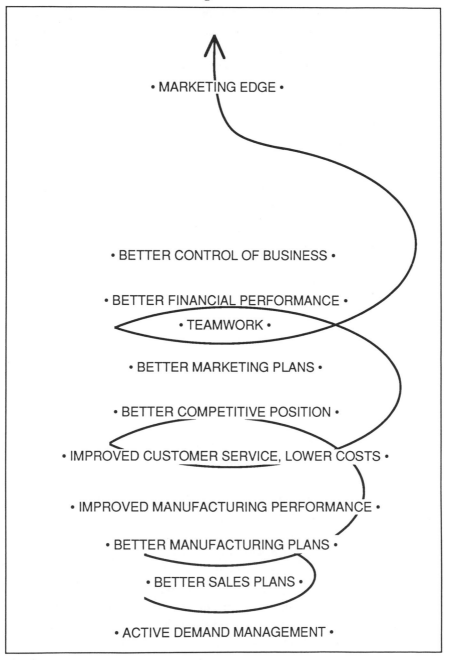

The upward spiral, led by active demand management.

In our experience, there are limits to the amount of change that can be expected in manufacturing's capabilities; it can change only so much, so fast. No matter how good or professional the manufacturing people may be, they can't do the impossible. One of the primary functions of demand management is to give manufacturing the visibility and time needed to provide the capacity and materials necessary to meet sales' and marketing's expectations.

Sales and marketing, because they are in closest touch with the customer, are responsible for providing this visibility to manufacturing. The following two case examples illustrate this point.

In the first, a sales organization of a garden equipment manufacturer on the West Coast expected an increase in business. It had no formal means of communicating this information to manufacturing to ensure that the appropriate products would be available to support the increased business. Their business plan had been set at the annual business planning meeting three months earlier. Although the salespeople had subsequently told their sales manager of their expectations for increased business, the sales manager and manufacturing manager did not meet regularly to discuss anticipated changes in business levels. Sometimes, this type of information *might* be passed along informally in hallway conversations. The increased business did materialize, but the company was unable to respond quickly enough to meet the demand, and the incremental business went largely to the competition.

In contrast, another manufacturer we're familiar with had implemented an MRP II system with an effective demand management system. This company's sales organization foresaw a significant increase in business. The anticipated increase was communicated to manufacturing during the company's monthly Sales and Operations Planning meeting, and the company was able to handle the increased business with minimal impact, problems, and frustrations—because manufacturing had the information it needed in time to adequately prepare for the increase. And, most importantly, they had happy customers.

End of the spiral? There's actually a subtle benefit that persists. As the company meets its production dates and financial targets, a new spirit of teamwork begins to permeate the organization. If sales and marketing people request better product lead times, manufacturing will work hard to improve them—because manufacturing understands the source of the need. Manufacturing people, in turn, might ask for more stability in the production schedule, and sales and marketing will work hard to provide that stability—because sales and marketing understand manufacturing's requirements. Corporate managers not only ask for changes in the business plan, but they actually achieve them as well! The bottom line is that with MRP II and active demand management, corporate management gains control of the business.

MRP and MRP II have been called many things, some of them in jest: Material Requirements Planning, Manufacturing Resource Planning, Miracle Requirements Planning, More Ridiculous Priorities, etc. After Bently Nevada first became a Class A MRP II manufacturer, we believed MRP meant *Marketing Runs the Place.* But it truly means Management Runs the Place, together, as a team.

This principle was illustrated nicely at a specialty chemical processor that had been a sole source supplier to several airplane manufacturers. Prior to implementing MRP II, this company's own management characterized the business as "on the way to the grave," given its reputation for poor customer service. Its customer service performance level at that time was 54 percent. Customer service levels were determined by the percentage of time the product was available when the customer requested it. In a period of three years, after MRP II went on line with an active demand management process, events took a very different turn. Customer service increased to a very respectable 97 percent, sales increased by 85 percent, raw material inventories plunged by 42 percent, and staff levels dropped by 19 percent.

What was the real secret behind this manufacturer's success? According to several top managers, once everyone understood the concept behind MRP II, sales and marketing stopped fighting with manufacturing, and all the organizations began working towards the shared goal of improved customer service. Each percentage point that customer service improved spurred people to work even harder, which resulted in a very strong and viable company that will surely be one of tomorrow's leaders in the field.

CRUCIAL DIFFERENCES

In addition to the obvious difference between the company on the downward spiral and the company skyrocketing toward world class performance, there are several other important benefits in utilizing a resource planning system with active demand management.

1. *Control over product availability.* The name of the availability game is "control." The company on the upward spiral is able to identify products and product lines for which stocking levels are inadequate or the product lead times are unacceptably long. The ability to monitor and correct unacceptable availability is crucial to remaining competitive.

One maker of outdoor furniture proved this principle when it decided that a product lead time of six weeks was far too long for it to be competitive. The company was constantly losing business even though it had a quality product that was reasonably priced. After implementing MRP II, it found that it always had sufficient capacity and the right parts, so it was no longer plagued by shortages. Marketing provided input on anticipated demand, and the company was able to make its standard product available in less than one week. As a result, it wound up taking business away from its leading competitor.

2. *A confident sales force.* The ability to deliver product when promised is a vital credential for a salesperson—it leads to a trusting relationship with the customer. A firm with a formal Manufacturing Resource Planning system and active demand management should be able to consistently achieve the necessary finished goods availability and/or on-time delivery to be competitive. A company without such planning systems is "winging it," and its sales force spends time making excuses instead of booking new orders.

A key element for any salesperson is confidence that the company will support his or her efforts. If the company repeatedly fails to deliver a certain product on time, a seasoned salesperson will often simply refuse to sell the product line, rather than jeopardize old and trusted relationships or get new ones off to a bad start. For instance, we talked with a veteran medical instruments salesman who had managed to maintain a positive attitude throughout the years even though the company he worked for experienced continuous delivery problems with different product lines. When asked why he was always so positive, the salesman replied, "I don't sell anything that isn't available. If I know the company is having delivery problems with a certain product,

I wait until the problems have been fixed before selling the product. Why create headaches for my customer and myself?'' As this salesman's comments illustrate, when salespeople avoid selling products, the company doesn't have a delivery problem for long.

A similar situation happened at the Ilsco company, a manufacturer of electrical connectors, when only 20 percent of its products were shipped on time. Everyone, from the salespeople to the sales management to the president, spent an inordinate amount of time explaining to customers why their orders were late. When the company employed MRP II and Just-in-Time (JIT), customer complaints stopped. The company president, who on a typical day would handle two or three irate customer calls, now received no calls at all from unhappy customers. The company's vice president of marketing noticed the difference, too. "It's sort of like being a Maytag repairman," he said.

3. *Smoother product introductions.* Traditionally, engineering designs new products, then hands them off to manufacturing for production, much like a relay race. Unfortunately, if the designs call for a sub assembly or component that has a lengthy lead time, the finished product might be a long time away. As a result, sales and marketing will have to wait an additional period of time before the product is introduced or available for delivery to customers. Customers, of course, will also be waiting—we would hope.

In contrast, the company on the upward spiral uses its communications and resource planning system for improving the "time phasing" of product development activities. For example, components or materials with long lead times can be purchased in parallel with the overall engineering product design effort. This reduces the total product development cycle, making the product available to sell earlier. Sales and marketing can help in this regard by providing a *time phased* forecast of anticipated demand and ensuring that the company is using time phased resource planning. This active role may help the company to exploit significant marketing opportunities.

One maker of microprocessing equipment used a time phasing approach to new product development and found that its on-time customer deliveries of new products shot up from 51 to 95 percent. One of the managers responsible for the resource planning system later commented that the on-time delivery improvement meant the difference between "a hot new product and a dust gathering failure."

4. *Ability to respond to change*. Most businesses operate in an environment of continual change, and survival depends on the company's ability to anticipate and respond to that change. The popularity of some products wax and wane over time, and customers' ordering patterns change with their own internal needs.

Within a company, too, change is certain. A quality problem may be discovered that requires significant engineering changes. A competitor's latest introduction may cause a product to become obsolete. A component vendor may go out of business or drop a product line. Or marketing may request engineering changes that make a product suitable for a wider marketplace.

A company on the upward spiral has the control and flexibility needed to meet changing customer demands. Such a company recognizes that its sales and marketing organizations are closest to the customers, and should therefore have the lead role in "taking the temperature" of the marketplace and regularly communicating customer needs to the rest of the company.

A comparison of two companies illustrates this concept. Company A was modifying one of its key products to include a safety feature requested by many of its customers. This particular company had no MRP II or formalized demand management system. The production control department scheduled the phaseout of the original product and the phase-in of the modified product based on its best guess of what the demand would be. The basis of the guess was the history of demand for the old product. What they did not anticipate was that the competition did not offer this safety feature, and companies that formerly purchased from their competitors were now interested in buying their product. Knowing of the improved product, the sales organization assumed the modified product was available in quantity immediately and began selling it with vigor to current and new customers. But, in fact, the product would not be available for weeks, and a poor customer service situation plus an inventory problem with the original product resulted. Further, the sales organization criticized the factory for being "out of touch with the real world."

In contrast, when Company B introduced a new, more technologically advanced product that would make obsolete a product the company had sold for three years, it had an effective control system in place, with sales and marketing actively participating. The engineering, manufacturing, and sales organizations agreed to a phase-in and phaseout schedule, which resulted in the sales organization selling the original product until the new product was available and promising the new product only for delivery in the future. The result? Happy customers and virtually no obsolete inventory.

5. *A single game plan, based on the same set of numbers.* A Class A Manufacturing Resource Planning system allows top managers to review and analyze revenues, costs, sales, bookings, production output, inventory levels, backlog/delivery lead times, product availability, customer service, demand, forecast accuracy, and business assumptions—from a single set of numbers. The company's operating numbers tie into the financial system so that all of the company uses the same set of numbers to manage the business. This leads to a better understanding of the company's relationship to the marketplace and better communication between all departments. One set of numbers helps all departments to operate following the same company game plan.

TURNAROUND TOOLS

In order for a company to ascend along the positive spiral of success, certain fundamental processes must be in place. The underlying framework for these processes is MRP II, a set of planning and scheduling tools that takes advantage of the power of the computer to link customer requirements with the rest of the company. Demand management is the means through which sales and marketing provide their input into the Manufacturing Resource Planning process. Once data about the marketplace are integrated into the resource planning system, management and manufacturing have the necessary information to develop support plans throughout the company.

In addition to MRP II, companies continuing on the upward spiral must also operate with a Just-in-Time (JIT)/Total Quality Control (TQC) philosophy, which enables them continually to eliminate waste and improve performance. They may also use Distribution Resource Planning (DRP) to enable themselves to manage distribution demands. MRP II, JIT/TQC, and DRP are discussed in depth in appendix A. Since demand management is of central importance to this discussion, we'll take a closer look at it in the following section.

Before we proceed, we'd like to stress that even if your company does not presently use the management tools mentioned above at this time, don't close the book; although a formal system must inevitably be brought on line in a growing company, you can help your company begin an upward spiral by demonstrating the vital need for these tools and spearheading an implementation effort. We firmly believe that companies that have gained operational control through a demand-driven, formalized Manufacturing Resource Planning system combined with JIT/TQC will be the most competitive, and perhaps the only survivors, in the long run.

DEMAND MANAGEMENT

During the past decade, major efforts to improve manufacturing performance have been undertaken by many manufacturers. Efforts have been expended to implement MRP II, JIT/TQC, and automated design and manufacturing processes, which has resulted in a general upgrading of the manufacturing profession. These improvements have largely been in response to global competition and the attendant requirements for survival.

What is unfortunate, however, is that most of the effort has been expended in the manufacturing or supply side of the business. Surprisingly little effort has been expended to better understand and communicate the *demand* side of the business. To achieve long-term competitive success, a company cannot simply work the supply side of the issue. Sooner or later, it must address the demand side. Fortunate are those companies that address the demand side early as they strive to improve their manufacturing capabilities, because, as we have stated earlier, manufacturing is ultimately demand driven.

It has been our experience that as a company improves its manufacturing capabilities and performance, inevitably a problem surfaces related to sales and marketing. Here's what happens. Company management is quick to realize that better visibility of demand and better understanding of the business are required by *all* departments to achieve continued improvements in performance. At this time, the sales and marketing organizations receive much attention, usually with the goal of improving the forecast. Because they are a key link to continuous improvement, sales and marketing are forced to step up to this responsibility and more. When addressing the demand side of the business, it quickly becomes apparent that the issue is more than just improving the forecast. It encompasses the entire subject of demand management.

The need for demand management was recognized by the the American Production and Inventory Control Society (APICS) in 1979, when it first published a definition of demand management:

> "The function of recognizing and managing all of the demands for products to ensure that the master scheduler is aware of them. It encompasses the activities of forecasting, order entry, order promising, branch warehouse requirements, interplant requirements, interplant orders, and service parts requirements."

Another way to describe demand management is to define it as the process of ensuring that the demands upon and capabilities of the company's manufacturing resources are in sync with each other.

Today, more than ever, companies must do an excellent job of managing demand if they are to achieve their objectives. We know, from a manufacturing perspective, that MRP II can greatly enhance productivity and efficiency. As we mentioned earlier in the chapter, though, for MRP II to reach its maximum potential, it must be driven by active demand management. Since marketing and sales are responsible for knowing the market and are the organizations closest to the customer, it is clearly their responsibility to take a leadership role in the demand management process.

There are an estimated ten thousand MRP systems in operation in the United States today; however, only approximately five hundred companies have reached Class A MRP II status. (MRP II users are rated from Class A to Class D.) While nearly all companies realize significant benefits from MRP, Class A MRP II users have achieved the maximum results from their efforts.[2] In analyzing the reasons why most companies are not achieving Class A status, it is apparent that input from sales and marketing and top management to the Manufacturing Resource Planning process is often lacking. Without such input, MRP systems tend to become manufacturing systems rather than *company* operating systems.

Obviously, the company exists to support customers, and since sales and marketing are the closest to the customers, it is their responsibility to form a cooperative effort with manufacturing by providing information on anticipated demand in a way that can be used effectively by manufacturing and management.

Demand management performed by the sales and marketing organization serves to ensure that customers' needs are satisfied while simultaneously stabilizing demand for the company's manufacturing, engineering, and other support organizations. This enables them to improve their performance in regard to customer expectations. Without demand management, these organizations are handicapped in their efforts to provide a quality product at a low cost, and deliver them on time.

To demonstrate how your company can gain a marketing edge through demand management, this book will address in subsequent chapters the following major issues:

- *Marketing/manufacturing strategy* for achieving customer expected availability and delivery lead times, considering the lead times required by manufacturing to produce the product.

- *Sales and Operations Planning* for operating the company based on one game plan and one set of numbers.

- *Sales planning* for gaining commitment to sell the plan.

- *Forecasting* for bridging anticipated demand with the factory schedule.

- *Master Production Scheduling* for turning plans into reality by managing demand to promise and meet customer delivery dates.

---

[2] A survey conducted in 1985 by the Oliver Wight Companies provides details on the types of results companies have achieved through MRP programs.

CHECKLIST

As you read through the book, you'll learn how each area contributes to anticipating and servicing customer demand. In the next chapter, you'll learn how sales and marketing can share their insights into customer demand with the rest of the company, and how to mesh these assessments of demand with those of upper management. Once you start thinking and communicating in such terms, you'll have taken a major leap in helping your company achieve new standards of performance.

Before going on, take a look at the following checklist—it just might serve as a catalyst for analyzing your company's current approach to demand management:

1. Is your company satisfied with the current level of customer service, and is it sufficient to keep you competitive in the future?
2. Do company departments work together as a team? Or do they work apart as antagonists?
3. Do sales and marketing think of manufacturing as the competition?
4. Do you use management tools, like MRP II/JIT/TQC, to bring about the total success of the company?
5. Does your company have a clearly defined demand management process?
6. Do sales and marketing lead the demand management process?
7. Does your company's application of active demand management involve continuous monitoring of changes in the marketplace and a formal means of communicating these changes to management and manufacturing?
8. Do sales, marketing, and manufacturing act hand in hand to manage demand and efficiently and effectively adjust production to satisfy customer and company objectives?
9. Do sales and marketing also work with engineering to ensure that new products are introduced as swiftly as possible by including them in the resource planning processes?

Chapter 2

Beyond Forecasting: The Leadership Role of Sales and Marketing

Plans are nothing; planning is everything.
—**Dwight D. Eisenhower**

MAGIC NUMBERS

Almost every company has an annual business planning process in which financial targets and budgets are set for the following year. Whereas this process is important for establishing goals and communicating a company's expectations for the following year, these business plans are often not sufficient for *running* the business.

In some companies, business planning is a fairly short process, and the plan is developed without a tremendous amount of detailed analysis. The resulting numbers are then used for the annual financial plan, and for the generation of pro forma statements for the financial community. These numbers serve as goals or targets for the company as a whole, but lack sufficient detail to be used as operations plans.

In other companies, a great deal of time and energy is devoted to the annual planning process and the development of numbers. The selling and marketing organizations do extensive planning for the year, and top management leads the overall planning processes with its goals and expectations. At the end of this process, an annual plan is generated, which is used by finance for its plans and communication with

23

the financial community. These numbers are also used to develop the company's operation plans.

Although the extensive planning approach sounds obviously superior, it may be counterproductive if it takes a number of months to complete. Let's say that the company's fiscal year runs from January through December. The various departments might begin their planning process in September of the preceding year. As a result, the numbers that are used to develop the annual plan are often unreliable, for even as the plans are being made, significant changes can occur in the marketplace. The company that requires excessively long planning times, like the company that rushes its planning process, may wind up with numbers that do not reflect market conditions being used to create production and other departmental plans.

For example, one electronics component supplier that is working on improving its operations planning process recently told us how its sales force and marketing organization spent a significant amount of time coming up with a detailed product forecast. This forecast was used to drive the manufacturing and product development plans for the company for the next year. The forecast was developed in September for the following fiscal year. Beginning in October after the annual plan was completed, but prior to January, there were significant changes in the competitive situation in the market; one competitor had dropped out, and another had introduced a technically superior product. As of January, the forecast developed nearly three months earlier was obviously out of date, but it was still used by manufacturing in planning capacity and materials. Not surprisingly, manufacturing wound up with excess capacity in some areas and insufficient capacity and materials in other areas.

Another problem associated with the lengthy planning process is departmental reluctance to change an annual plan, especially if they have gone to a great deal of trouble to gather and crunch the data. This tends to reduce the amount of updating that occurs, which makes the numbers less useful in a changing marketplace. When the plan is not updated frequently, communication of essential information is reduced within the company, and the company becomes less flexible and responsive.

A plan that is updated infrequently is a plan that does not reflect reality. Even if the "magic numbers" do coincide with the gross revenues, the *product mix* and the *timing* of the incoming orders may be poorly anticipated, which will have a definite impact on a company's performance.

For example, let's say that a company had a fairly disciplined planning process, the primary purpose of which was to develop financial plans. Unfortunately for this company, very little information regarding the product mix and timing of the orders was communicated by sales and marketing to manufacturing. One year, the actual product mix was extremely different from the anticipated mix, and manufacturing found itself unable to respond. Even though the question "What are we going to *sell?*" was answered accurately in terms of gross dollars, the company was unable to *ship* product. And because the financial performance was based on shipments, not on bookings, the company missed its overall financial targets.

In another year, the same company did a much better job of forecasting the product mix and again hit the gross dollars selling target fairly closely. But a large portion of those sales were actually booked in the last part of the year, and the orders could not be shipped during that fiscal year because of manufacturing's lead time. Once again financial performance to plan suffered even though the dollarized selling goal had been met. But in each case, the resulting financial performance was not as originally planned; the company hit the selling target but missed the financial goal.

GROUNDED IN REALITY

Progressive companies have come to realize that they must have a process in place that enables them to identify, communicate, and respond to change in a timely manner. Even more important, they must anticipate change and have contingency plans in place to accommodate those changes if they occur. Many companies manage change effectively through a formalized process called Sales and Operations Planning.

Whereas the traditional annual financial plan is developed and updated during the year, usually on the basis of the company's fiscal calendar, an updated company operations plan is reviewed regularly, at least on a monthly basis, through Sales and Operations Planning. The latter is necessary, since the nature of the marketplace is constantly changing, and companies must continuously adapt to those changes. If the marketplace is particularly volatile, or an unusual event takes place, the company's operations plans may have to be updated even more frequently. A retired Coca-Cola executive pointed out the inadequacy of a once-a-year plan recently when he said, "I used to be able to plan and hit my financial targets and budgets without a problem. I certainly don't see how I could do it today. With all the changes in the economy and marketplace, it seems to be an almost impossible task."

For example, consider a consumer goods company that must update its plan once a week as the Christmas buying season approaches. If that company misses the Christmas window, it loses its sales opportunities for the year.

Or consider what can happen if a major new customer agrees to buy your product. You might be blessed with a flood of unexpected orders. If you don't have a system for effectively communicating current and future customer demands to manufacturing, you may not be able to meet the new demand and continue to satisfy your old customers at the same time. Again, what a lost opportunity! The key concept is to have a formalized process to communicate changes in demand: Sales and Operations Planning.

OPENING A WINDOW ON THE FUTURE: SALES AND OPERATIONS PLANNING

Sales and Operations Planning is the process whereby the management of the company provides direction, resolves conflicts, and manages the operations of the business. It is the tool that links the business plan to the more specific objectives of the organization. The Sales and Operations Planning process ensures that all the divisions, departments, and other organizations within the company are pulling in the same direction at the same time toward the same goals.

During Sales and Operations Planning, opportunities and problems are reviewed and specific plans are agreed upon. Since Sales and Operations Planning occurs on a regular basis, it ensures that the entire company has an ongoing, up-to-date plan at any time.

The inputs to the Sales and Operations Planning process come from the functional managers in the company. A typical Sales and Operations Planning process starts with a statement of anticipated demand, provided by sales and marketing through a demand planning process. The company's resources are then reviewed to see how the company can meet the demand. Manufacturing confirms that the necessary capacity and materials are available to meet the sales plan; engineering confirms that the design resources are available to meet anticipated new product introductions and changes in existing products; finance agrees that the fiscal resources are available to carry out the plan; and corporate management confirms that the plan is consistent with the overall corporate objectives.

The outputs of the Sales and Operations Planning process are specific sales and manufacturing plans, which establish the rates of sales and production. The process is used to develop financial plans for the planning horizon and to identify capital resource requirements. Since these plans are developed directly from the plans of the functional managers, they more closely model reality. The output of the process is one game plan, one set of numbers, for the entire company.

With Sales and Operations Planning, the management team of the company meets on a regular basis, at least once a month, to review past performance, anticipated demand, current position, and business assumptions and expectations by *product family*. Management then agrees upon the forward-looking sales plans and production plans for each family. These plans cover an agreed-upon planning horizon, typically twelve months or longer. Not only are the sales plans and production plans reviewed and agreed upon, but also the support plans for the other functional areas of the company are reviewed and agreed upon as well. These plans include new product plans, engineering plans, quality plans, maintenance plans, and so forth.

The Sales and Operations Planning meeting is attended by the CEO (or general manager) and his staff. Participants usually include the

Figure 2.1

The first Sales and Operations Planning meetings are sometimes difficult, especially if attendees come unprepared.

managers of sales, marketing, finance, manufacturing, materials, engineering, human resources, quality, and other support organizations as appropriate.

"Now hold on," you might argue. "If we got everybody together in one room and tried to make them agree on a game plan, we'd have the biggest barroom brawl this side of the Mississippi!" Perhaps so, and your company wouldn't be alone in this regard (see figure 2.1). The solution is to make sure that differences are resolved as much as possible *before* everyone gets together, so that the Sales and Operations Planning meeting is a process of *refining* the game plan and ironing out minor differences. The CEO then acts not only as a contributor, but also as a referee and arbiter in the process, so that consensus is reached with the least possible pain and waste of energy.

One of the major benefits of Sales and Operations Planning is that it eliminates most surprises regarding the financial performance of the company. It makes potential problems visible early so that solutions can be developed before company performance and customer service are affected. A complete review of the Sales and Operations Planning process would be beyond the scope of this book; to learn more about it, see *Orchestrating Success* by Richard C. Ling and Walter E. Goddard.

The Sales and Operations Planning process provides the sales and marketing organizations with a great opportunity to influence and control the direction of the business since the output of the process is the company's operational plan. This process starts with a forecast of anticipated demand, as input by sales and marketing.

Some companies consider the forecast of anticipated demand and the sales plan as being one and the same. There is a distinct difference between the two, however. A forecast of anticipated demand is an estimate or prediction of what customers will ask you to deliver during your planning horizon, and is based on a review of history, external and internal indicators, market segment conditions, promotional strategies, pricing considerations, and assumptions made about the future of the company's marketplace. It is normally communicated in the Sales and Operations Planning process by product line.

In contrast, a sales plan is what the sales organization has committed to sell. It is supported by individual sales objectives, customer and territory plans, market channel plans, and product plans. It is usually stated by customer or territory with target accounts and action plans formulated to reach the sales objectives. The Sales and Operations Planning process starts with a forecast of anticipated demand, which becomes the company sales plan when sales commits to sell the plan.

Once the sales plan has been established, the discussion centers around how the company will meet the sales plan. Will manufacturing require additional tooling or assemblers to meet the plan? Will sales require additional salespeople in particular territories to garner the business? Will marketing need to develop a direct mail program or advertising program to attract new customers? Manufacturing will be eager to participate in this process, for it benefits from the improved visibility and

Figure 2.2
Forecast of Anticipated Demand

		1	2	3 ——————▶	12	Total
Family	$	88,000	88,000	88,000 ——▶	88,000	1,056,000
	Units	160	160	160	160	1920
Product A	$	25,000	———————————————————▶			300,000
	Units	55				660
Product B	$	25,000	———————————————————▶			300,000
	Units	45				540
Product C	$	38,000	———————————————————▶			456,000
	Units	60				720

A forecast of anticipated demand in units and dollars.

communication of anticipated changes in demand. They can order and install the tooling and hire and train new assemblers in advance rather than scramble at the last moment. And the end result for sales and marketing is that, with proper preparation, the rest of the company directly supports their sales and marketing objectives.

PREPARING FOR SALES AND OPERATIONS PLANNING

Marketing's role

Sales and Operations Planning is driven by demand, and therefore starts with the development of a time-phased forecast of anticipated demand. Marketing is responsible for developing this forecast. Some companies have established a position of demand manager or demand planner (under a variety of titles) to administer this function. (The role of the demand manager will be discussed later in the book.)

A useful forecast projects customer orders in terms of product, quantity, and *timing* (see figure 2.2). The minimum planning horizon for projecting demand is typically twelve months, but depending upon the company's business cycle, it may be twenty-four months or longer.

The key factors that determine the planning horizon are: (1) the cumulative lead times for manufacturing the product; (2) the lead time for obtaining materials and components, including visibility for vendor negotiation; and (3) the amount of time required to make significant capacity changes.

As you can see in figure 2.2, the forecast shows units and dollars as a function of time. Now let's take a closer look at the major types of information communicated in the forecast of anticipated demand:

What products the customers need.

For the purposes of the Sales and Operations Planning process, the customer's needs are described in terms of product lines or classes. This is typically presented in terms of product "families" by which the company defines its business. Quantities need to be communicated in both units and dollars.

How much product the customers need.

Quantity is defined in terms of dollars for financial purposes, and units for manufacturing purposes. The units might be individual items, pounds, gallons, or some other unit of measure, depending on the nature of the product. Note that this unit breakdown is one of the major benefits in helping the factory prepare for production.

Where the customers need product.

In many businesses, the issue of "where" the product is needed is as important as "what," "how much," and "when." Immediate availability of a company's products for customers is a primary reason for distribution systems. For those companies that have distribution networks, it's necessary to forecast where the product is needed.

Forecasts of anticipated demand are created by using historical forecasting techniques, reviewing the company's marketing and sales plans, looking at other demand streams on the company (such as interplant demands, service and spare parts, and distribution), reviewing product pricing and promotion plans, and generating and documenting assumptions about the future of the company's marketplace.

When the customers need product.

Timing is one of the key elements of a forecast, and anticipated demand needs to be communicated in time-phased arrays. This is necessary for manufacturing to schedule both materials and capacity, for the essence of Manufacturing Resource Planning lies in having valid schedules.

Of the elements of forecasting described above—"what," "how much," "where" and "when"—determining "when" is typically the most difficult task. The company doesn't wish to make products earlier than necessary, as this would tie up resources that could be used to service other customers. The flip side, of course, is that customers don't want the company to produce the products later than necessary.

For example, at Bently Nevada we had a product line that was easy to forecast for annual quantity, but extremely difficult to forecast for timing of required deliveries. In this situation, we had to work with manufacturing to develop a strategy for both communicating the forecast and responding to actual demand when it arrived. It took some time before manufacturing and marketing understood that orders coming early in the year didn't necessarily mean we should increase the forecast and, conversely, that a small number of orders early in the year didn't mean we should reduce the forecast.

The Sales Organization's Role

Every professional sales organization does sales planning. This is required to ensure that sales has proper coverage of its customers, territories, and markets. Sales planning is actually used for capacity planning within the sales organization—how many salespeople, representatives, and/or distributors will be needed to carry out a particular volume of business? Sales planning is also used to develop a budget that covers anticipated salaries, commissions, bonuses, and expenses necessary to hit the sales objectives.

When the sales planning information is shared with the marketing organization, marketing can use the information to confirm that the plan is realistic and consistent with its forecast of anticipated demand. Alternately, marketing may use the sales planning information to modify its forecasts. We should note here that the structure of sales and marketing organizations varies from company to company. In some companies, both sales and marketing come under the direction of one manager. In other companies, they are separate organizations managed by two different people. Whatever the structure, however, the sales and marketing functions remain essentially the same.

The objective of preparing a recommended sales plan is to enable the sales organization to develop a plan that it will stand behind in terms of accountability and responsibility. In other words, the sales organization will say to the rest of the company, "This is what we plan to sell. If you can support it, we'll turn the sales projections into customer orders." (The details of creating a sales plan are discussed in chapter 5.)

ACHIEVING A CONSENSUS BETWEEN MARKETING AND SALES PROJECTIONS

Once marketing has developed a forecast of anticipated demand and sales has developed a sales plan, the two organizations must compare the numbers to see if they concur. Typically, there will be differences between the two plans in terms of quantity, timing, or product mix. The differences need to be reconciled by the two organizations working together as a team, with the end result being one plan agreed upon by both the marketing and sales organizations. If consensus can't be reached, upper management will have to arbitrate the dispute.

To simplify the process of gaining consensus, marketing and sales should communicate in the same product families or groupings over the same periods of time and in the same units. If the two organizations have not agreed upon a formal structure of product families, they will be talking in different languages. For example, it is not uncommon for sales organizations to plan their sales by customer in dollars. Marketing, however, forecasts by product in dollars and units, and will have to translate the sales organization's dollar plan into products and units in order to communicate with the manufacturing organization in the Sales and Operations Planning process.

Note that during this part of the demand planning process, sales and marketing are not operating in a vacuum. There are communications with upper management about the numbers and the progress, and upper management will have made its expectations clear to both organizations. As a result, sales and marketing will not only be striving for a consensus between the plans they generate, but will be attempting to reflect management's goals as well. If management's plans are too ambitious or conservative, sales and marketing will have to voice their opinions. In any case, sales and marketing and management must ultimately agree upon a plan.

Understanding Management's Biases

Just as sales and marketing will differ in their outlook on the marketplace, upper management has its own concerns. Often, management has a bias toward increased business. A natural tendency is therefore to set company objectives higher to ensure that the company will stretch itself to meet management's expectations. In some cases the stretch will be beneficial, stimulating people to go the extra mile. In other cases, though, the sum of the product lines' forecast simply cannot meet the expectations, and the conflict will have to be resolved. Failure to resolve the conflict will guarantee serious problems as actual customer demand falls behind the company's (management's) sales plan. Assuming manufacturing is building to the plan, inventory will increase, financial projections will be missed, and company performance (profit) will falter.

A company in the Northwest believed it had a problem with the forecasting department, and asked for an evaluation of its situation. Something was definitely amiss, because sales performance consistently fell behind plan. Further analysis of the situation revealed that the sales organization was meeting sales objectives for all product lines except one. The product line in question was new, and it had been forecasted for by the company's president. The forecasting department had repeatedly warned that the introduction plan for this product was highly optimistic. Nevertheless, the forecast was left unchanged, and manufacturing built to meet the plan, resulting in significant buildup of inventory to the point where the company had to acquire additional warehouse space. It took management some time to recognize that the forecasting problem was its own, not the forecasting department's.

Documenting Assumptions

Given the potential for different perspectives on the business, it is very important for each department to document the assumptions used in its decision-making process. If all departments document their assumptions, differences will be much easier to resolve. Perhaps management might see steady growth over the past few years and extrapolate a number. In the current year, however, sales and marketing know that because of certain changes in the marketplace, the extrapolation is unrealistic. Or it might simply be a situation in which top management is pressured by the shareholders for a certain ROI, and announces that the target figures must be X, Y, or Z. The onus is then on the heads of the sales and marketing organizations to prove *why* and *how* X, Y, or Z can or cannot be attained.

The reverse situation can also occur, in which management *lowers* the levels that sales and marketing are projecting. Let's say that the sales and marketing organizations of a fiscally conservative company see new opportunities for expanding the company's market share. To do so might require expensive promotions and additional plant capacity that management is unwilling to fund. As a result, management may request sales and marketing to lower its projections in keeping with management's financial strategy. In any event, the sales and marketing and management teams must agree upon the revised expectation of anticipated demand, for it is the basis of the company's Sales and Operations Planning (see figure 2.3).

Seeing Eye-to-Eye with Manufacturing

Once sales and marketing have an agreed-upon forecast of anticipated demand that meets management's expectations, it needs to be

Figure 2.3
Demand Planning Process

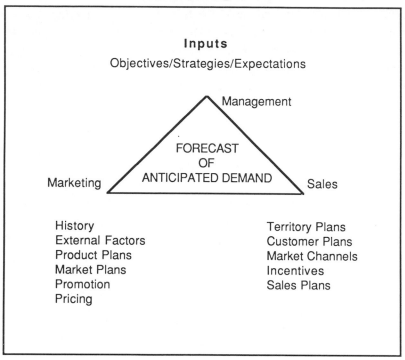

The forecast of anticipated demand drives the company's Sales and Operations Planning process. This forecast is developed by achieving consensus between marketing, sales, and management.

communicated to manufacturing so manufacturing can prepare formal production plan recommendations for allocating resources to meet the expected demand. It is important for sales and marketing to communicate the forecast to manufacturing far enough ahead of the monthly Sales and Operations Planning meeting for manufacturing to perform "rough cut capacity planning" to determine if they have sufficient capacity to meet the anticipated demand. Given enough information and time to perform rough cut capacity analysis, manufacturing will be prepared to present alternatives in support of the demand at the Sales and Operations Planning meeting. The forecast of anticipated demand is also communicated to engineering and finance and other support organizations, so that they can be prepared for the formal Sales and Operations Planning meeting.

Early Sales and Operations Planning meetings at Bently Nevada were difficult and sometimes less than productive because the different departments did not appropriately communicate prior to the meetings. In far too many meetings, the marketing organization would come in with a surprise change in the forecast, and manufacturing was expected to advise whether they could support the changes. Without time to evaluate the situation, manufacturing would have to "wing it." Sometimes their answers would be accurate, sometimes they wouldn't. As the process at Bently developed, we greatly improved the pre-Sales and Operations Planning communications between departments.

Major problems are likely to be encountered when sales and marketing arrive at the Sales and Operations Planning meeting unprepared. As we mentioned, at Bently marketing at first came in to the meeting with surprise changes in the forecast of anticipated demand. But at least they were prepared. At other companies we have seen sales and marketing forecasts of anticipated demand change *during* the Sales and Operations Planning meeting. When this situation occurs, the credibility of the forecast and the sales and marketing organizations is seriously impaired. Coming into the meeting with an agreed-upon forecast of anticipated demand increases credibility and reduces second guessing by other attendees.

DEMAND PLANNING SESSIONS

To prepare for the Sales and Operations Planning meeting, companies conduct demand planning sessions. The marketing organization generally conducts the demand planning session a few days prior to the Sales and Operations Planning meeting. The objectives of the sessions are to:

- Develop unified marketing forecasts and sales plans with recommended adjustments, if needed, to existing sales plans for presentation at the Sales and Operations Planning meeting.
- Identify and discuss major projects or anticipated large orders that are not considered part of the baseline sales plan—known

as abnormal demand—and develop strategies to manage this
demand.

• Identify changes in key leading indicators and external factors
and discuss their impact on the sales plan.

• Identify changes in trends that may indicate necessary adjustments in sales plans for product lines.

• Identify changes in product line mix and options, and identify
the causes for these changes.

• Analyze major competitive developments that may affect sales
plans.

• Discuss new product introduction plans, product enhancement
plans, product obsolescence plans, and changes in pricing or
promotional strategy that may impact sales plans and product
mix forecasts.

• Identify and document changes in assumptions that underlie or
support the sales plans.

Who Should Attend Demand Planning Sessions?

Because the primary objective of the demand planning session is to
present a strong, unified recommendation at the Sales and Operations
Planning meeting, the demand planning sessions should be attended
regularly by sales managers, customer service managers, marketing
and sales executives, product managers, distribution managers, major
account managers, market segment managers, and the demand planning staff. It also can be helpful if the sessions are attended by the
master scheduler to facilitate communications with manufacturing. This
way, the master scheduler hears what changes are being made without
having to wait for a written communication.

Each person attending the sessions contributes his and her unique
perspectives to the demand planning process. For instance, product
managers can explain shifts in product line mix or option mix. They
can also be expected to provide direction as to why sales plans should
be changed because of the impact of new product introductions, promotional programs, and pricing changes. Major account managers help
plan or explain abnormal demand from large users, original equipment
manufacturers (OEM's), or distributors. Customer service managers

and the master scheduler use their insight and experience to identify discrepancies in demand from the original sales plan. Market segment managers convey key changes in demand for given markets and popularity levels of product lines within their segments.

Distribution managers contribute their knowledge of inventory levels and demand patterns, which are key factors in developing and adjusting sales plans, to help determine what products manufacturing needs to produce and when products are needed. Distribution managers also help determine changes in product mix or inventory objectives that will affect forecasts and sales plans. In addition, they assist in developing distribution strategies required to satisfy demand.

THE SALES AND OPERATIONS PLANNING MEETING

Individual plans come together in a formally scheduled meeting, which is attended by representatives of *all* departments and is chaired by the general manager. During the Sales and Operations Planning meeting, any discrepancies or conflicts in the plans will be worked out, and, if necessary, revisions will be made to the recommendations of the individual organizations.

If the demand can be achieved without any problems, the Sales and Operations Planning meeting may be over quickly. But if there are difficulties meeting the volume or timing required, the meeting becomes a session for resolving conflicts. During the session, manufacturing should present alternatives, such as overtime, extra shifts, farming out some manufacturing to outside firms, and other maneuvers that require management's approval. However it is achieved, consensus on a company plan must be reached by all attendees.

In the process of determining the production plan, given the company sales plan, there are two key elements that need to be reviewed and managed: inventory and backlog/customer lead time. (Backlog is defined as all orders entered but not yet shipped.)[3]

---

[3] "*Backlog* traces its origins to the American frontier. Pioneers, who did not enjoy the luxury of matches, were faced with the necessity of maintaining an uninterrupted fire for months at a time. They solved the problem by placing a large green log in the back of the fireplace. Even when dry wood burned out, the green log, or backlog, always provided enough smoldering embers to start a new fire. This backlog seldom was used for fuel but was available as an emergency reserve." *American Way*, August 5, 1986.

The amount of backlog directly affects the customer delivery lead times. The greater the backlog, the longer the lead times, and vice versa. Given a specific sales plan, by setting the production plan either greater than or less than the sales level, inventories and or backlog/lead times can be increased or decreased. Having said that, one must truly use time-phased backlog presentations to understand customer lead times. And it is at the Sales and Operations Planning meeting that inventory levels of finished goods and backlogs are actually managed. The responsibility for the management of inventory and backlog rests with the Sales and Operations Planning meeting attendees, who represent each organization in the company.

Both inventory levels and customer lead times are of primary concern to sales and marketing, since they have a direct impact on customer service. Both organizations need to participate actively in the Sales and Operations Planning process or they will abdicate customer service to others in the company. In some companies, like Black and Decker and Xerox Corporation, sales and marketing actually ''own,'' and thus manage, the finished goods inventory. It is clearly sales' and marketing's responsibility to manage the levels of finished goods inventory through their requests to manufacturing for product.

AFTER THE SALES AND OPERATIONS PLANNING MEETING: THE ONGOING WORK

Once a consensus has been reached on the company sales and production plan at the Sales and Operations Planning meeting, the results are published and distributed to the rest of the company. The minutes of the meeting should include (1) sales plans and production plans by product families and (2) any anticipated changes to the business or financial plans.

At this point, the production plan, which started off as family and product groupings in monthly time frames, will have to be broken down into specific products at specific dates for manufacturing to build. This is done by the master scheduler, who creates a manufacturing plan at the detail level (called the master production schedule) for each product based on *detail* item forecasts from marketing. (How to communicate detail forecasts to the master scheduler so they can be turned into detailed production plans, will be discussed in greater depth later in this book.)

Besides converting the families and time periods into more detailed units and time frames for production, sales and marketing must translate the sales plan into specific sales plans, by territory, salesperson, and product lines. In fact, the real work has just begun! As soon as the numbers are published, the sales and marketing organizations must turn their plans into reality. Because of revisions at the Sales and Operations Planning meeting, the sales organization might have to work with distributors to increase the volume of certain product lines. Marketing might have to go back and reinforce those lines with adjustments to the marketing mix, additional promotions, product enhancements, price adjustments, or other measures.

If the plan calls for increased sales, additional marketing promotions or some additional sales coverage may be required. Conversely, it may require some change in pricing or delay of promotions to sell only the agreed-upon plan.

As time progresses, marketing must continuously monitor actual customer demand and compare it with the sales plan, noting differences. Marketing will be required to point out any significant deviations from the sales plan at the next Sales and Operations Planning meeting, or possibly at a special session if the situation warrants it.

It is important to reinforce the idea that the Sales and Operations Planning process does not stop with the first meeting. Unlike the annual business planning session, Sales and Operations Planning provides ongoing direction to the entire company at *every* Sales and Operations Planning meeting. These meetings must be conducted at least monthly to assess changes to anticipated demand and adjust production accordingly. As in the case of the first Sales and Operations Planning meeting, the sales and marketing organizations must do their homework to determine the needs of the marketplace, and to corroborate with manufacturing and engineering that the plans can be achieved. In essence, once the Sales and Operations Planning process has been initiated, it becomes an integral process within the company and never stops.

WHY DO SALES AND OPERATIONS PLANNING?

Having just read this chapter, you might think about all the meetings and premeetings and ask, "Doesn't this take time and energy? And is it worth it?"

The answer is yes to both. We've already talked about the enormous benefits of setting up communication channels among the various organizations. As for the energy and effort, there's no denying that the first time you do Sales and Operations Planning, it will require a good deal of effort; most companies find it a significant job to pull together numbers that have never been assembled before, and to get agreement from people who may consider themselves to be internal competitors or adversaries.

To be sure, though, as your company gets better at anticipating demand, its Sales and Operations Planning meetings and the attendant preparation will become easier and eventually will require less time. No major benefits in business are free—they take a lot of energy, preparatory work, and communications. The result, though, is the ability to gain *control of the business* and to use manufacturing as a competitive weapon.

CHECKLIST

1. Is your company's annual business plan used to drive the operational plans of the company? Or is the business plan just a financial target for the year?
2. Does your company have a Sales and Operations Planning process, driven by anticipated demand? Is the forecast of anticipated demand provided by marketing and sales?
3. Do marketing and sales conduct a pre-Sales and Operations Planning session to identify problems and opportunities and resolve differences in preparation for the formal meeting? Do sales and marketing agree on the company sales plan? Or do they operate under a different set of numbers and objectives?

Is the plan given to manufacturing prior to the Sales and Operations Planning meeting so that manufacturing can prepare a production plan?

4. Is the resulting sales and production plan used to develop the company's financial plans? Or must finance "magically" adjust the numbers?

5. Are manufacturing and sales and marketing responsible and accountable to perform to the Sales and Operations plan?

6. Do your forecasts of anticipated demand include what products the customers need, how many they need, when they need the products, and where they are needed? Are the forecasts of anticipated demand developed by the sales and marketing organization? Are the forecasts updated regularly to reflect the current situation?

7. Is there consensus with top management on the company's sales plan? Or does management operate under a different set of expectations?

8. Do you have regular communications between sales and marketing and manufacturing to ensure there are no surprises?

9. Are the company's sales and production plans supported by detailed action plans?

Chapter 3

Developing a Marketing/ Manufacturing Strategy

The meek may inherit the Earth—
but they won't grab any market share.

—Anon.

WHAT DO YOUR CUSTOMERS EXPECT?

The first step in turning manufacturing into a competitive weapon is to develop a marketing/manufacturing strategy that meets customer needs and takes advantage of your company's manufacturing capabilities. Without first developing an agreed- upon strategy, effective communications between marketing and manufacturing are hampered. Both marketing and manufacturing must reach agreement on the company's basis for competition, especially as it relates to customer delivery lead times. Often, conflicts will crop up between marketing's expectations and manufacturing's capabilities. To compete effectively, these expectations and capabilities must be balanced.

For example, a manufacturer of electronic control systems experienced a reduction in business, though the market for its product was growing. Upon analyzing the situation, it was obvious to the sales organization why orders were being lost. The competition was offering two-to-three week delivery lead times, while their company's lead times were fourteen to sixteen weeks.

A closer look at the situation revealed that manufacturing was operating under a make-to-order strategy, in which parts were purchased and all manufacturing was performed *after* receipt of an order. The company believed that carrying any inventory was risky, expensive, and wasteful. Unfortunately, the competition had elected to carry inventories of subassemblies and only had to assemble the product after receipt of a customer order. This example illustrates how the expectations of the customers (two-to-three week delivery) was out of balance with the company's capabilities (fourteen-to-sixteen week delivery). Once the company recognized its significant competitive disadvantage and understood how its marketing/manufacturing strategy was contributing to that disadvantage, the company elected to change the strategy to build to a sub-assembly level and finish to order. This change in strategy reduced the company's lead time and made it competitive.

The first question that must be answered in developing a marketing/manufacturing strategy is "What are the availability and delivery lead-time requirements of the customer?" Notice we did not say, "What are the lead times in manufacturing?" The starting point is demand, and therefore we must understand demand before we build a manufacturing strategy to support it. The next question to answer is "What is the cumulative manufacturing lead time (time from purchasing materials through finished product)?" The final questions to answer are "What are the conflicts between customer requested lead times and the company's cumulative manufacturing lead times?" and "Where do manufacturing lead times exceed customers' expectations for delivery?" Figure 3.1 presents a sample format and definitions for analyzing lead times.

A successful marketing/manufacturing strategy must take into account the difference between customer requested lead times and manufacturing lead times. In considering these differences, a key objective of a marketing/manufacturing strategy is to maintain flexibility by not committing your resources until the last possible moment. In other words, whenever possible, do not finish a product before it's needed. In any situation, if the cumulative manufacturing lead time is greater than the amount of time the customer gives you to deliver the product when he places an order, you must produce all or some of the product in advance. Consequently, you have a period of uncertainty when you are required to build to a forecast of anticipated demand, as illustrated in the following case.

Figure 3.1

Marketing/Manufacturing Strategy
Lead Times Analysis

	Competitive Delivery Lead Times	Customer Requested Delivery Lead Times	Customer Delivery Lead Times	Cumulative Manufactury Lead Times	Percent Emergency Business
Product 1	3-4 Days	3-4 Days	6-8 Days	6 Weeks	11%
Product 2	1-2 Weeks	1-2 Weeks	1-2 Weeks	2 Months	2%
Product 3	3-4 Weeks	2-3 Weeks	5-7 Weeks	4 Months	4%
Product 4	5-6 Weeks	2-4 Weeks	4-5 Weeks	4 Months	Nil
Product 5	8-10 Weeks	8-10 Weeks	8-10 Weeks	6 Months	Nil

Lead Time (LT) Definitions

Competitive Delivery LT: The customer delivery lead time offered by the competition.

Customer Requested Delivery LT: The average time after placement of an order that customers are asking for receipt of the product.

Customer Delivery Lead Time: The length of time from order placement until receipt of product by the customer.

Cumulative Manufacturing LT: The total length of time to fabricate the product, including acquisition of materials, tooling, etc.

Percent Emergency Business: The percent of the orders that are requested by customers to be shipped immediately with minimal concern for cost.

Example of lead time analysis for marketing/manufacturing strategy.

A customer gives you a purchase order with an eight-week delivery requirement. Your cumulative manufacturing time to build the product is twenty weeks. Therefore, twelve weeks before receipt of the purchase order, you need to place orders for the materials and, perhaps, partially complete the product if you are to meet the customer delivery requirement. The objective is to commit the materials and labor to produce at the last possible moment, but still meet the customer request date. Otherwise, you may build items that you might not be able to sell. In addition, you may have used material and labor to build inventory instead of servicing a customer order.

If you can stay flexible—get the base materials you need, perhaps partially complete the product, and then finish the product to a customer order—you improve your ability to respond to demand. Sales and marketing need to influence the manufacturing organization in order to gain the most practical level of flexibility. However, those companies whose finishing process takes longer than the customer allows for delivery will be forced to make the product to 100 percent completed state, i.e., they will need to make the product to stock to meet customer delivery requirements.

The following case illustrates the type of thinking that must occur to develop a flexible marketing/manufacturing strategy. A company manufactures modern gasoline pumps. This product is a combination of mechanical assemblies, electrical assemblies, computerized communications hardware and software, and external packaging. Through an analysis of demand, the company sees that its customers would be satisfied with a delivery lead time of three to four weeks after placement of their purchase orders.

An analysis of the company's manufacturing lead times reveals that the cumulative manufacturing lead time is approximately twenty weeks, which obviously, if the company is to respond to the customers' requested deliveries it needs to begin the manufacturing cycle in advance of receipt of purchase orders. How much material should the company buy? What parts should be built? Manufacturing's production and inventory control departments are responsible for answering these questions, but they require information from sales and marketing to answer the questions as correctly as possible. Sales and marketing, which should be responsible for being closest to the customer, contribute their knowledge of customer expectations with a forecast of anticipated demand. Armed with this knowledge, the production and inventory control departments can determine more reliably the strategy needed to meet customer expectations.

The company must decide how far through the manufacturing cycle it should proceed before receipt of a customer order. Some of their alternatives are:

1. Finish the product completely.
2. Complete major sub-assemblies.

3. Complete minor sub-assemblies.
4. Purchase material only.

This decision will be based on how much of the product can be completed in less than the customer requested lead time (three to four weeks). If the company can complete the entire product from purchased material in this time, the company gains the greatest flexibility. The more the product can be completed after receiving the order, the greater the flexibility.

Sales and marketing want the greatest possible flexibility since their forecast of anticipated demand will not be 100 percent accurate, especially at the detail level. The total volume of product may be fairly easy to predict. The total number of variations, however, may be impossible to forecast accurately. If the products are built to their finished configuration, the company may literally have to disassemble and reassemble the product to meet specific customer order requirements.

MANUFACTURING ALTERNATIVES

Some of the alternatives to consider in developing a manufacturing strategy that best meets both customer delivery requirements and manufacturing lead time requirements are:

1. Engineer-to-order.
2. Make-to-order (including finish-to-order and/or assembly-to-order).
3. Make-to-stock.

What's the best strategy for your company? The following examples illustrate some of the factors to be considered in determining which strategy will work best for you.

Engineer-to-Order

If you're in a market situation in which your customers give you all the time you need, you really have a reduced need to forecast—you know what customer orders are coming in the door. While most businesses do not have this luxury, those that do are often in engineer-to-order (ETO) environments. Defense contractors for new airplanes or ships are good examples of ETO businesses. It is usually economically unfeasible for these businesses to stock finished goods in the hopes that a customer will place an order. In many cases, ETO companies literally start with the design of the product, then proceed through procurement, manufacturing, and assembly—after receipt of the customer purchase order.

Engineer-to-order businesses, however, still must do forward planning to ensure that sufficient capacities will be available to accept future contracts. Usually, companies find that they are not 100 percent engineer-to-order and must actively forecast and manage demand to meet *all* customer commitments.

Make-to-Order

In a make-to-order (MTO) environment, the customer may allow sufficient time for procurement of materials and the manufacture of the product after placement of the order. For instance, let's say you're selling safety instruments for a nuclear reactor. The design engineering has been completed, perhaps on another contract. But the company has not purchased any materials in anticipation of an order. The materials used in this product are specified differently from the manufacturer's standard product line; chances are, they would have to be radiation-resistant materials. In an MTO setting, you would avoid buying these expensive special materials until you've received an order. As a result, the delivery time to the customer will not include the time to engineer the product, but will include purchasing time through final assembly time.

In another make-to-order situation, the customer may not allow sufficient time for procurement of materials, but will allow some delivery lead time. In such instances, finish- or assemble-to-order are viable alternative strategies. This means the product must be partially completed prior to receipt of an order. A finish-to-order or assemble-to-order strategy is often used when the manufacturer elects to compete on the basis of offering a large number of product options. Rather than trying to stock all items with all options, which would be costly and very difficult to forecast, the manufacturer builds common subassemblies in advance, completing the final product after specific customer orders are received. The advantage is improved flexibility with a reduced risk of creating unusable inventories.

Make-to-Stock

Some customers simply will not allow sufficient lead time after receipt of an order to complete the manufacture of the product. Companies that serve such customers must use a make-to-stock (MTS) strategy. Products are manufactured to their final configuration (stock keeping units—SKUs) and placed in inventory in anticipation of customer orders. This approach is necessary for immediate, "off-the-shelf" delivery.

Obviously, if you have many product variations, this strategy can be costly when particular options or variations do not sell, and they sit on the shelf until they become obsolete. In many cases, by analyzing actual customer requested lead times and reviewing the manufacturing process, there are opportunities to change from a make-to-stock strategy to a more flexible, make-to-order strategy. When this is accomplished, greater flexibility and better responsiveness to the customer can be achieved while maintaining the same or reduced levels of inventory. There is also a greatly reduced potential for inventory obsolescence.

After analyzing customer expectations, many companies find that distributed inventories are required for immediate availability and to reduce transportation costs. It is possible to have a distribution marketing strategy with distributed inventories of finished goods while simultaneously having a make-to-order (finish-to-order) strategy. By establishing agreed-upon delivery lead times to distributors, the manufacturer can structure the product so it can be completed after the distribution centers order the product. An excellent "tool" for implementing a distribution strategy is Distribution Resource Planning (DRP), which will be discussed in chapter 7.

There are many examples of companies that have successfully converted a product from a make-to-stock to a make-to-order strategy. One manufacturer of office furniture and office systems has been very successful at making this shift. The company offers an almost infinite variety of options to the customer—color, fabric, material, etc. After analyzing its customers' requirements (including distribution) and the company's manufacturing capabilities, the company elected to adopt a finish-to-order manufacturing strategy. In order to adopt this strategy, the manufacturing organization had to streamline its final assembly operation so it could finish the products within the lead time expected by the customers. Forecasting has been streamlined as well, since sales and marketing do not need to forecast end item configurations by specific time period, which became an almost impossible task. With the finish-to-order strategy the company maintains maximum flexibility by enabling its manufacturing organization to finish its products according to specific customer orders rather than building products to finished goods inventory.

One of the product lines at Bently Nevada was electronic transducers. Customers expected delivery of transducers within a few days after placing an order, and often same day delivery was requested. After Bently first implemented MRP II, we elected a make-to-stock strategy. Our customers bought variations in type, diameter, physical length, and cable length, so after we decided upon the SKUs for finished goods, we had to forecast and build sixteen hundred different transducer models.

It took us a few months to realize that we were unable to forecast accurately the mix of so many different products, so we began to fill a warehouse with inventory. Much worse, we found we were unable to meet customer expectations for delivery because we had the wrong items in inventory, and we began to lose business to the competition.

We reviewed the problem with manufacturing and decided to change from a make-to-stock to a finish-to-order strategy. This new strategy required manufacturing to change its production process by shortening the finishing cycle. We ended up forecasting approximately forty items, and manufacturing produced subassemblies that were completed after receipt of customer orders. This change in strategy made forecasting considerably easier. Most importantly, though, customer delivery dates were met 95-plus percent of the time, while inventory levels were reduced substantially.

WHERE DO YOU MEET YOUR CUSTOMER?

Every manufacturer has an opportunity to view his customer requirements in the light of his current manufacturing strategies. Richard C. Ling, of R. C. Ling Inc., and an Oliver Wight Education Associate, refers to this as determining "where you meet your customers." Current manufacturing strategies at most companies have evolved without specific analysis or an explicit strategy formulated by management. As a result, most companies are rife with opportunities to gain flexibility, improve customer service, minimize inventories, and improve demand planning simply by taking the time to analyze their present position (see figure 3.2). Companies that involve marketing, sales, manufacturing, and management in this process may find widely varying perspectives on the current marketing/manufacturing strategy.

Consider a small motor manufacturer, for example. In a group discussion of where the company meets its customers, the marketing manager thought the company was or should be make-to-stock because customers were constantly expediting orders and asking for earlier delivery dates. The manufacturing manager believed the company should be operated under a make-to-order approach since there was always a significant backlog of customer orders. After more closely analyzing customer delivery requirements, it was determined that for the principal product lines, customers would accept a lead time of two to three weeks—*if the company shipped the orders on time*. Armed with this information, the company implemented a finish-to-order strategy in which it completed the motors after receipt of customer orders. As a result of this plan, the company realized tremendous benefits in terms of improved customer service and reduced inventory.

It is often desirable to use both make-to-stock and make-to-order strategies within the same product lines. One company charges full price for immediate delivery, but gives a discount when customers allow a lead time to manufacture or finish the product. Other companies indicate in their catalogs which products can be shipped immediately and which products they're prepared to make but require a longer lead time for delivery. Still other companies give customers a price

Figure 3.2

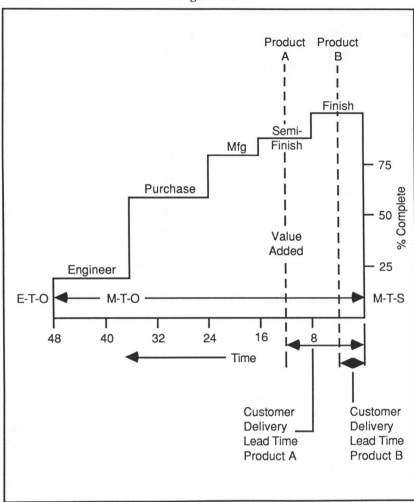

Where do you meet the customer? In this example, the customer delivery lead time for Product A allows more flexibility and more time than for Product B.

break for ordering designated standard optional items. Finally, some companies maintain an inventory of key products for emergencies and unexpected opportunities, but manufacture most of the products after receipt of an order.

In the process of determining where your company meets its customers, the marketing and sales organizations have the responsibility of honestly determining what delivery lead times will be competitive for which product lines. With knowledge about these lead times, they then can communicate and work with the factory to allow it to implement a manufacturing approach that will satisfy customer requirements, and at the same time provide manufacturing flexibility. A few key points about this process should be kept in mind:

1. Customer lead time requirements will vary by product line
2. Customer lead time requirements may vary by market segment and even by customer within product lines.
3. There's a tendency to establish lead time objectives based on a small frequency of occurrences. Let's say, for example, that 95 percent of the time, customers are satisfied with a four-week lead time for a particular item. Five percent of the time, however, emergency situations arise and customers expect a lead time of one week. It is inappropriate to establish a one-week lead time objective for that entire product line, and the temptation to do so should be overcome. To be sure, the 5 percent emergency orders need to be addressed, but not by setting unnecessary objectives for the entire product line.

To accommodate emergency orders, sales and marketing and manufacturing must formulate an emergency plan before emergencies happen. One company we have dealt with recognizes that emergencies are a significant part of their business, and plans and allocates material and capacity in advance just for critical situations. Sometimes, by a previously established policy, an emergency is automatic authorization for top priority and special handling. This means that the routine customer delivery schedule may have to be altered to meet the emergency demands. At Bently Nevada, we had an agreed-upon set of rules for handling this type of order. Our customers had a top-level priority when their machinery was out of service, and we did everything possible to help customers in these situations. If a customer placed an emergency order with us, it became a "ROMADO" (*ro*tating *ma*chinery *do*wn—top priority).

When a ROMADO occurred, manufacturing had a number of options for getting the product to the customer immediately. It could work overtime, use premium air freight, and, as a last resort, could change the delivery schedule of other customer orders. But it did so after conferring with the sales department to determine which orders could be rescheduled. In other words, manufacturing had a heavy club at its disposal to meet emergency orders, and marketing had the right to set the ROMADO priority, but both were used with great appreciation of the aftershocks a ROMADO could cause.

These aftershocks were the many previously scheduled customer orders that were caused to be late as a result of giving another order ROMADO priority.

TIME FENCES

In the process of evaluating your company's present situation, it's important to understand the flexibilities and inflexibilities inherent in your current manufacturing process. When we refer to "manufacturing flexibility," we mean the ease or ability to adjust to change. When we consider the ability to change in relationship to time, we would expect that almost any changes can be made in the distant future within the constraints of capital resources. If you want to make changes to the plan outside the cumulative manufacturing lead time, presumably the only changes you have to make are in capacity, since materials have yet to be ordered. The point in time at which such changes can be easily made is referred to as a planning "time fence" (see figure 3.3).

In conversations with many marketing and sales people, it is not unusual to find a lack of understanding of the need for time fences. Sales in particular typically believes that manufacturing should have the capability to respond to any customer demand immediately without previous notice. This would be true in an ideal world, in which the cost of manufacturing still allowed for competitive pricing. In reality, it takes time to acquire materials, increase capacity, and manufacture the product. The establishment of time fences is simply a recognition of that reality. We encourage sales and marketing to reduce the amount of time it takes to acquire material, increase capacity, and manufacture the product, but until they do, it is necessary to recognize the real world constraints.

Figure 3.3

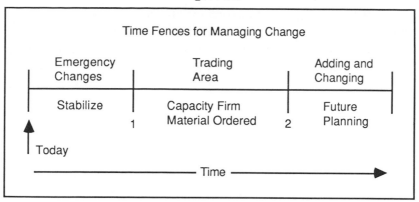

The points which define windows of change to the plan are referred to as "time fences."

Perhaps sales and marketing can better appreciate the situation if the following question is raised: how much can you change your booking rate instantaneously? Assuming you are aggressively pursuing the market today, a request to increase sales by 20 percent next week is probably out of the question. A request to increase sales by 20 percent next year, however, may be entirely realistic. The same concept of time fences thus applies to sales and marketing as it does to manufacturing.

As you move closer in time, you begin to commit your resources into more and more specific product configurations. This begins to limit your degree of flexibility to make changes. For example, once material has been purchased, it may not be possible to increase the plan significantly. Inside the planning time fence, sales and marketing need to work in concert with manufacturing if changes are to be made. Changes in product mix can often be made at this point, but changes in overall volume become increasingly difficult to make.

Still closer in, we encounter a point at which manufacturing has begun the final completion of the products. Here, it becomes extremely difficult to change one product into another, and the volume of output is nearly fixed. In this area of the time line, changes usually get made either at great expense or at the risk of compromising customer satisfaction, because some other customer orders may have to be rescheduled to accommodate the change. Once again, there must be an agreement between sales, marketing, and manufacturing about how to make changes at this point. In the establishment of a marketing/manufacturing strategy, time fences need to be determined by individual product. This will facilitate communications and the identification of products that may be in a risky competitive situation. It will also stimulate a review of specific marketing/manufacturing strategies for these products.

The traditional use of the expression *time fences* is somewhat misleading, as it sounds like a *wall* for sales and marketing. In fact, time fences are merely indicators of when changes can economically be made. They are decision points relative to change. They should be respected, but they aren't sacred. A clear understanding of what each fence means is therefore critical for accommodating necessary changes without jeopardizing customer service and profitability.

MEETING CHANGES IN DEMAND

Even though customer lead time objectives, marketing/manufacturing strategy, and time fences have been determined and agreed upon, changes in market conditions will cause customer lead time requirements on individual products to be missed. When this happens, marketing and manufacturing must work together as a team to satisfy customer lead time needs and requirements. This team effort will center around two different approaches, which can be used alone or in combination.

1. *Improve the forecasting of the products in question.* By paying greater *attention* to the particular product lines, you can get a better picture of anticipated demand. Forecasts will improve, and changes in production will be fewer and of smaller consequence. Further, necessary changes can be determined and communicated *earlier*, giving manufacturing more time to respond.

2. *Reduce the company's internal lead times.* If time fences can be moved closer in, the company can respond more quickly to changes in demand. Flexibility and competitive responsiveness will also be in-

creased. To reduce cumulative manufacturing lead time (the total time from purchasing materials through completion of a finished product), you must first conduct an analysis of those areas that require *time*.

It has been said that "time is the enemy." So the key to better customer service and an improved ability to compete is to reduce the time it takes to manufacture products. That, however, is only part of the picture. Whereas manufacturing is often the longest lead time, other lead times need to be reviewed, including those associated with forecasting, planning, engineering, purchasing, suppliers, order entry, and distribution. If it takes a long time to communicate changes in the forecast, manufacturing can't begin to take the necessary action to change production (e.g., ordering parts, tooling up, scheduling capacity, etc), or, consider order entry as a source of lead time.

A manufacturer of capital equipment found that after working to reduce its manufacturing lead time, some of the products could be manufactured (assembled-to-order) in less time than it took to clarify and enter the customer purchase orders. The customers considered the company's lead times to be too long, and they didn't care whether the logjam was in manufacturing, engineering, order entry, or distribution. The company acted swiftly. It increased order entry capacity, eliminated queues, and streamlined procedures to slice order entry from two weeks down to *two days*. Now that's a reduction in lead time!

At this point, you may recognize that the whole process of reducing lead time is part of an approach described earlier: JIT, the continuous and relentless elimination of waste. In fact, reducing lead times is one of the key items in implementing JIT/TQC.

When the efforts described above still fail to satisfy customer lead time requirements, it becomes necessary to review the fundamental marketing/manufacturing strategy once again. This review should start with an analysis of customer demand. There may have been significant changes to the expectations of the marketplace relative to lead times. The competition ultimately sets the delivery lead times, so lead time changes are a primary stimulus for review of marketing/manufacturing strategies. In fact, it is necessary to regularly update and review your marketing/manufacturing strategy.

CHECKLIST

1. Have you analyzed your customer's delivery lead time requirements by individual product line?
2. Have you established a marketing/manufacturing strategy for individual products or families? Is flexibility a major consideration?
3. Have time fences been established, agreed upon, and revised as needed by manufacturing, sales, and marketing working as a team?
4. Do you review your customers' delivery lead time requirements on a regular basis to adapt to changing customer expectations?
5. Is there an ongoing effort to improve the demand planning/forecast process?
6. Is there an ongoing effort to reduce your company's lead times?

Chapter 4

The Fine Art of Forecasting

The rule on staying alive as a forecaster is to give 'em a number or give 'em a date, but never give 'em both at once.
—Jane Bryant Quinn

BRIDGING ANTICIPATED DEMAND AND THE FACTORY SCHEDULE

Even though you may have the best marketing/manufacturing strategy and the best Sales and Operations Planning process in the world, you won't be fully in control until you link anticipated demand with your manufacturing execution system. This linking process begins with forecasting and passes through the various stages of demand planning, including sales planning, until it reaches the Master Production Schedule, which specifically defines what products manufacturing is to build.

As we mentioned in chapter 1, demand management is the process of ensuring that market demand and the company's capabilities are in sync. Demand planning includes those functions that allow the company to prepare for anticipated customer orders. It links with Sales and Operations Planning, as described in chapter 2. Demand planning includes developing forecasts of anticipated demand, sales planning, customer linking, demand stream management, and contingency ("what if?") planning.

In this chapter, we'll discuss how to develop forecasts, the differences in various types of forecasts, different users of forecasts, and common forecasting problems. Chapter 5 will discuss sales planning and explain how sales planning and forecasting work together in the development of demand plans. Chapter 6 will be devoted to Master Production Scheduling.

FORECASTS: WHO NEEDS THEM?

Before we get into the specifics of the forecasting process, let's explore who uses the forecast, and assess their needs:

1. Senior managers need to be aware of potential demand, so they can evaluate their options with regard to the business. For example, when provided with a picture of the *potential* marketplace, "unencumbered" by current constraints, they will be in a better position to make long-term decisions about such items as growth objectives and capital expenditures. The marketing organization has the responsibility of providing senior management with a forecast of total market demand, for use in the company's strategic planning process. Through the strategic planning process, market share objectives are established. These objectives provide guidance for the development of business plans, which then link to Sales and Operations Planning.

In the Sales and Operations Planning process, senior management needs a time-phased forecast of anticipated demand for the planning horizon, typically twelve months or longer. This forecast is used to establish the company's production rates, as well as the inventory and backlog levels required to support the company's customer service objectives.

2. Sales management needs forecasts to assist in preparing and updating their recommended sales plans as input into the Sales and Operations Planning process.

3. Manufacturing needs the aggregate sales plan stated in units. This information is an output of the Sales and Operations Planning meeting. Since the Sales and Operations Plan addresses only product families or groupings and rarely addresses all of the individual items contained in the Master Production Schedule, manufacturing also needs a time-phased forecast of product mix. A product mix is a statement of the probable

"popularity" of each part number within each Sales and Operations Plan family.

4. Finance needs an aggregate shipments plan stated in dollars, which is also an output of the Sales and Operations Planning process. This shipments forecast is used for financial planning and will often differ from both anticipated demand and production in terms of timing.

5. Engineering, quality assurance, and all support organizations require a forecast of future demand in order to plan for necessary resources. The Sales and Operations Planning process is designed to provide this information for these organizations as well.

TYPES OF FORECASTS

It may appear from examining your users' needs that there is no single forecast that satisfies everyone, but actually a number of forecasts used by different people for different purposes. Through the demand planning process, a time-phased forecast of anticipated demand is developed. This forecast is used in the Sales and Operations Planning process, which translates it into the company's sales plan when the company agrees to support the plan. The company sales plan can be presented in different ways for the different people, or functions, who use the plan. The key point is that all of the users will base their individual action plans on the company sales plan developed through the Sales and Operations Planning process.

Here is a brief description of the most common types of forecasts.

Forecast of Market Demand

This forecast could be called a statement of "pure" market demand. It is a forecast of potential market demand in its most unencumbered form, that is, unencumbered by internal constraints. This forecast represents what a company could sell if it had no limitations on capital, capacity, trained personnel, etc. Its purpose is to guide senior management in making "macro" decisions about the size and capitalization of the firm.

With this type of forecast, the idea is to project the demand that is only constrained by the available marketplace (market size and economic conditions), but not constrained by limitations on your ability to serve it. This forecast gives you a baseline for discussions and decisions regarding desired market share and your marketing/manufacturing strategies for achieving it. It thus serves as a reference for the development of the annual business plan, which then links to the Sales and Operations Planning process.

This kind of forecast is typically stated in dollars by major product line, market, or product families, usually over a three-to-five year planning horizon.

Forecast of Anticipated Demand

With the market demand forecast as a reference, you must develop a time-phased forecast of anticipated demand. The forecast of anticipated demand is based upon three elements: (1) projections of what customers will ask you to deliver during the planning horizon (what you will sell), (2) your company's internal constraints, and (3) your company's market share objectives. The difference between the forecast of market demand and the forecast of anticipated demand is that the forecast of market demand gives you the market's raw potential. The forecast of anticipated demand provides your company's portion of the market's raw potential.

The forecast of anticipated demand is expressed in terms of product, quantity, timing, and location (as applicable). This type of forecast answers the following questions: what, how many, when, and where? It is also sales' and marketing's input into the Sales and Operations Planning process. Since the forecast of anticipated demand is updated monthly, it recognizes the changing nature of customer demand and provides a rolling forecast over the planning horizon.

For Sales and Operations Planning, the forecast of anticipated demand may be stated in either dollars or units, and ideally is expressed both ways. The forecast should meet the following criteria:

1. It should be stated in terms that senior management uses to think about the business. For example, products, customers, or processes.
2. If stated in dollars, it must be translatable into units.

3. The product families or groupings used must be easily converted into groupings or units that are used by sales and marketing for sales planning and by manufacturing for production planning.

For example, manufacturing primarily thinks about its manufacturing processes, around which it must plan its labor and machine utilization. Therefore, it would prefer to state its forecast in units or hours or other terms that can be used to describe its manufacturing capacity.

Marketing, on the other hand, tends to think in terms of dollars, customers, and markets. Accordingly, it will forecast and plan in those terms. It is sometimes necessary to provide a translation mechanism for converting marketing's terms into manufacturing terms if manufacturing is to take advantage of the marketing and sales forecasts. For example, sales may forecast dollars by product by customer, but manufacturing may plan in units or individual items. A translation will be required to change the forecast of dollars into units of production.

Product Mix Forecast

This is a forecast that further converts the forecast of anticipated demand from overall product families or groupings to specific items needed for the Master Production Schedule. In most situations, there will simply be too many Master Production Schedule items or options to manage at the Sales and Operations Planning level; nevertheless, they must still be forecast for manufacturing to effectively operate the Master Production Schedule. The master scheduler must know specifically what to produce and when it is needed. Such information is derived from the product mix forecast. Often, the mix forecast is based on a series of percentages of the family that is forecast at the company sales plan level (see figure 4.1.)

Some companies allow the manufacturing department to develop the product mix forecast, either because manufacturing has better historical records at this detailed level, or as a means of "self-defense" since no one else will do it. In contrast, we believe that the marketing department should prepare the mix forecast. It is marketing's job to be aware of promotions, new product introductions, pricing changes, and competitive situations that may cause the future mix of demand to vary significantly from historical experience.

Figure 4.1

Product Mix Forecast

Time Period		1	2	3	4	
Product Family	Q	100	120	150	150	Aggregate Forecast
	%					
Model A	40	40	48	60	60	
Model B	20	20	24	30	30	
Model C	20	20	24	30	30	Mix Forecast
Model D	15	15	18	22	22	
Model E	5	5	6	8	8	

An example of a product mix forecast, which uses a series of popularity percentages of the family forecast.

Remember that although mix forecasts are important, they are driven by the aggregate forecast at the Sales and Operations Planning level. If you have an inaccurate forecast at the aggregate level, you will not fix the problem with your mix forecast.

For instance, there was a period of growth in one of Bently Nevada's major product lines. At first, we did not recognize that it was an increase in business for the overall product line. We thought that we simply had a product mix problem. For a couple of months, we constantly changed our mix forecast to reflect a perceived change in product mix. That is, when one item had sales in excess of its forecast, we adjusted the mix by increasing that item and lowering the forecast of another. Soon, we received demands greater than the forecast for the items we adjusted down, and we no longer had any place to change the mix without adjusting the overall aggregate forecast. In reality, our product mix forecast was reasonably accurate. Had we recognized the increase in overall business, we would have provided a more effective communication to manufacturing, enabling it to better respond with much less frustration on our part.

Bookings Forecast

This is a statement of expected incoming customer orders, expressed in terms of when the company expects orders to be received.

Shipments Forecast

This is a statement of when the company expects to actually ship the booked customer orders (see figure 4.2). The shipments forecast is derived from the Sales and Operations Planning process, through agreement on the company sales plan, production plan, inventory levels, and customer order backlog levels.

In a pure make-to-stock environment, the bookings forecast and the shipments forecast are essentially the same, since customer orders are shipped immediately as received, assuming available inventory. In a make-to-order or engineer-to-order situation, a time lag occurs between the order booking date and the order shipment date, and the bookings plan and shipping plan may be different.

Care must be taken to ensure that communications on the time phasing of forecasts are clear. For example, the corporate controller of a manufacturer of recreational vehicles recently shared with us how he had developed financial pro formas, based upon a "sales" forecast from the sales organization. He used these pro formas to communicate with his bank. Later, however, the company could not meet its shipping expectations, even though the sales organization was exceeding its sales plan. In analyzing the situation, he found that the sales forecast had been a forecast of bookings, and many of the orders booked could not be shipped for a variety of reasons: problems with a key supplier, customers asking the company not to ship early, and credit problems with two key customers. Consequently, the financial plans as presented to the bank (based on a "sales" forecast rather than on a

Figure 4.2

Demand Versus Bookings
"Sales"

Time period	1	2	3	4	5	6	➡
MAKE-TO-STOCK (with inventory available)							
Bookings	123	137	143	111	109	134	➡
Demand	123	137	143	111	109	134	
Shipments	123	137	143	111	109	134	

Orders booked are shipped in the same time period.

MAKE-TO-ORDER (starting with no backlog) Lead time = 1 period (material and capacity available)							
Bookings	123	137	143	111	109	134	➡
Demand	0	123	137	143	111	109	134
Shipments	0	123	137	143	111	109	134

The shipments plan in the Make-to-Order example is offset by the lead time.

MAKE-TO-ORDER—with Split Shipments							
Bookings	0	0	1,000	0	0	0	➡
Demand	0	0	0	200	300	300	200
Shipments	0	0	0	200	300	300	200

Note the significant difference in timing of bookings and shipments.

Time-phased bookings, shipments, and demand (the quantity of a product *when* the customer needs it) may all be different. Be sure that manufacturing gets a forecast of anticipated demand and finance gets a forecast of anticipated shipments.

forecast of expected shipments) were in error, much to the controller's embarrassment.

Even though it appears you may have different types of forecasts and different users of forecasts, the objective is the same: to operate the business from a single company plan, initially driven by the forecast of anticipated demand, the key element in the process.

DEVELOPING THE FORECAST OF ANTICIPATED DEMAND— DIFFERENT VIEWS OF THE ELEPHANT

There's an old story about three blind men who were asked to describe an elephant. Each of the blind men was permitted to touch a part of the elephant's anatomy and then was asked to describe what it was that he felt. The first described the elephant as a rope; he had touched the elephant's tail. The second described the elephant as a tree, for he had felt one of the elephant's large, stocky legs. The third man described the elephant as a snake; he had felt the elephant's long, flexible trunk. The moral of the story is that different people, with different perspectives of the same situation, can come up with entirely different views. Each is individually correct, although none describes the situation completely. Nowhere is this more true than in the development of a forecast of anticipated demand.

It's been our experience that people with effective demand planning processes take advantage of "different views of the elephant" that various people in the company bring to their jobs. Typically, three major views are involved: management's, marketing's, and sales'.

Management views the business primarily with broad considerations for corporate objectives and strategies. Often, management sees the marketplace in ways that others in the company cannot. Its perspective is shaped by communications with the heads of other companies, through relationships with the management of the company's customers, and with the business community at large. All these create a unique mental image of the problems and opportunities facing the company. This image forms management's expectations, which are used in the development and communication of the forecast of anticipated demand.

For demand planning to succeed, sales' and marketing's forecasts must coincide with management's expectations and vice versa. Should sales and marketing develop a forecast that is significantly higher or lower than management's expectations, discussions will be needed to resolve the conflict. Some companies aptly refer to this as the "top down/bottom up friendly contention process."

A number of factors influence marketing's view of the future; one

Figure 4.3

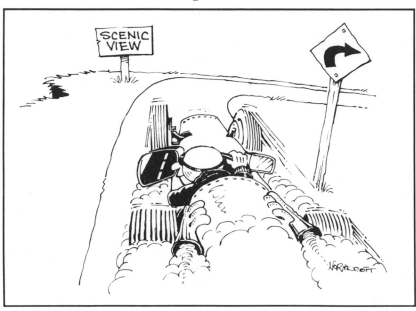

Using only history to forecast the future is like driving ahead, looking only into the rear view mirror.

important consideration is sales history. By looking at product sales over the past few years, marketing has a good starting point from which to develop its forecast of anticipated demand. History provides marketing with a starting level of business, information on seasonality, trends, and a foundation for product mix forecasting.

But history alone is insufficient for marketing to develop reliable forecasts (see figure 4.3). It must also use its knowledge of external factors that affect the business and internal marketing plans. External factors might include the economy, technology changes, competitive activities, the value of the dollar, and other considerations taking place outside the company. Internal marketing plans might include, among other things, promotions, pricing, new product introductions, and new market penetration plans. All of these factors need to be weighed when marketing develops a time-phased forecast of anticipated demand.

The sales organization's view of the market is extremely important in the demand planning process. Typically, the sales people are "closest to the customer" and often have the best current view of the marketplace. Consequently, their input is often more volatile than that of management or marketing but is extremely valuable in monitoring the company's customer base. Sales develops its perspective from its observations of customers and customers' plans, the establishment of sales territory plans, and from inputs observed in different market channels. The opinions of retailers, distributors, and original equipment manufacturers will influence the sales organization's perspective, as well.

An effective demand planning process takes all these different views of the elephant into account, reconciles them into one forecast, and documents the underlying factors and assumptions. The resulting forecast of anticipated demand is then used to drive the Sales and Operations Planning process, through which the forecast becomes the company's sales plan.

DOCUMENTING ASSUMPTIONS

In the process of reconciling the different views of the marketplace, it becomes apparent that different perspectives are often the result of different assumptions about the factors affecting the business. Forecasters and sales organizations are often criticized for poor forecasts when, in fact, their forecasts were reasonable considering the assumptions used in developing the forecast. A dedicated forecasting effort includes reviewing, understanding, and documenting assumptions about the factors that affect the business. This is the responsibility of management, marketing, and sales, and entails reviewing, understanding, and documenting the assumptions each has made about the business. When properly administered, forecasts are not wrong—they are inaccurate. *Assumptions* about the business are what prove to be wrong.

The process of documenting and reviewing assumptions has a number of benefits including:

1. Improved understanding of the business, the factors affecting the business, and how different organizations within the company view the business.

2. Improved communications among all people involved in the planning process.
3. Development of revised action plans to improve the company's performance when it becomes obvious that current plans will not be achieved.
4. Better understanding at all levels that forecasting is not a task that can be simply delegated and forgotten. The accuracy of forecasts is a function of sales planning and sales plan execution. This is a responsibility of management, not just of the forecaster.
5. Early warning of problems and early identification of opportunities.
6. The stimulus to perform "what if?" planning.

No one group—comprised as it is of people with different perspectives—will agree on all the assumptions, and it will wish to see different possible scenarios. But reviewing different scenarios soon leads to a better understanding of the marketplace and its sensitivities to various factors.

To illustrate how communicating the assumptions behind a forecast can improve the forecast's usability, think of the weatherman. In the days of radio and early television, the weatherman simply would tell the public whether it would rain, snow, or be sunny. The weatherman continuously proved to be wrong, and the public had little confidence in the forecast. In fact, the early weathermen gave the word *forecast* a bad name.

Later, the weathermen changed from giving an absolute forecast to providing a forecast with probabilities. For example, "There's a 75 percent chance of rain tomorrow." With the introduction of satellites and computers, the weathermen have begun sharing their information and their assumptions with the public. As a result, the users of the forecast not only have the weatherman's prediction, but also have a view of the factors behind the prediction. The weathermen may still not be absolutely correct, but the information they provide is more useful to the public as they try to develop future plans.

What Is Involved with Documenting Assumptions?

The process of documenting assumptions involves identifying and writing down the conditions and expectations that will have a major bearing on the company's demand and the company's ability to respond to demand. The documentation process takes place at both the strategic planning and product planning levels. Wherever significant decisions affecting dollars, unit quantities, or timing are made, major assumptions should be documented so they can be monitored for the unexpected. It is useful to categorize assumptions into two groups:

1. Those out of your control
2. Those within your control

Types of Assumptions

1. Conditions usually outside the company's control:
   a. Economic conditions (growth, depression, prime rate, new construction, currency exchange rate)
   b. Changes in technology
   c. Governmental action
   d. Global competition
   e. Market conditions
   f. Labor problems or strikes at suppliers or vendors
2. Items that, in theory, are within the company's span of control:
   a. New product development
   b. Promotions
   c. Sales coverage
   d. Distribution channels
   e. Capacity
   f. Product deproliferation (pruning)
   g. Product availability
   h. Financing

In addition to the categories of control, it is useful to organize assumptions according to product planning level:

1. Aggregate product level
   a. Market segment size and change
   b. Competitors' tactics
   c. Market seasonality

    d. Buyers' preference changes
    e. Available manufacturing capacity for different products
    f. Quality requirements and performance
    g. Product support availability
    h. Pricing effects and changes
2. Mix Level
    a. Industry standards
    b. Option preferences
    c. Effects of new or eliminated options or models
    d. Special promotions

It is not unusual to find people initially documenting assumptions as a defensive maneuver. In fact, the process often starts after a forecast proves to be significantly off base and the forecaster has been severely chastised. Certainly, this is not the best way to get going, but it is better than not starting at all.

The technique of documenting assumptions, when carried out in a positive way, can be a powerful decision-making tool. It ensures that more thought is put into planning and creates a sounder basis for review. And by fostering a better understanding of your business and what affects it, your response to the marketplace tends to become proactive rather than reactive. It therefore becomes crucial to the planning process that assumptions are reviewed, discussed, and either validated or changed as part of the monthly Sales and Operations Planning process (see figure 4.4.)

GETTING STARTED

In the forecasting process, *all* demand streams on the manufacturing resources must be considered. These demand streams include all of the demands that will be placed on manufacturing, engineering, and the support organizations. They also include demands from end-users or customers, distributors, original equipment manufacturers, repair parts, interplant requirements, samples, demonstration equipment, and internal plant needs. These demand sources must be considered to effec-

Figure 4.4

Not So Important	Important
1. What we make.	That we understand what we make better than anyone else.
2. That we work hard.	That we work smart.
3. That we like every-one we work with	That we respect those we work with and always consider their points of view.
4. That we land every quote we make.	That when we quote we offer our best timing, quality, and value.
5. That our forecasting be accurate with actual results.	That our forecasting be reviewed and measured against actual results, making us more knowledgeable of our markets and our products.

Curt Clarkson, President of The Clarkson Company in Sparks, Nevada, a manufacturer of valves and reagent feeders, provided this set of guidelines to his staff in a strategic session. Note guideline #5 on forecasting.

tively allocate materials and the capacity of your manufacturing facility, since all will compete for the same resources.

For example, the manager of forecasting and the master production scheduler for a midwestern manufacturer complained that even though they put tremendous effort into the forecasting process, manufacturing was not meeting their requirements. An investigation showed that two major sources of demand on manufacturing were not included in the forecast. These two major sources of demand were interplant demand from two other smaller facilities and component demand from the international division. These two demand streams accounted for approximately 23 percent of the business. Consequently, in order for the manufacturing department of this company to make realistic plans, it had to second-guess the forecast (product, quantity, and timing) to account for the missing 23 percent not included in the formal forecast.

In most companies, evaluating all demand streams is a full-time job. Traditionally forecasting has been the responsibility of market researchers, product managers, or forecast analysts. Recognizing the importance of demand management, some companies, however, have created a new position called the "demand planner" or "demand manager." We wholeheartedly support this concept and believe that other firms would do well to adopt it, too (see figure 4.5.)

We often find product managers responsible for forecasting, but the reality of their day-to-day activities precludes them from spending sufficient time on the forecasting effort. Typically, the product managers' daily activities are consumed by new product development, sales communications, promotions, technical communications with engineering, and shepherding target orders through the manufacturing facility. It's unusual for forecasting to receive more than a couple of hours of their time per month. The establishment of a demand planning function to administer the forecasting task, and to work with the product managers, the sales organization, and management, has proven to be effective in developing and improving a company's forecasts.

The function of demand planning is important, and we caution against placing it too low in the organization. We have seen companies with forecasters who performed their job very well, but lacked the clout to influence upper management or to question upper management's plans when they were obviously not achievable. The titles for the demand planning function vary in different companies. Some of the titles we have seen used include: demand planner, demand manager, sales planner, manager of Sales and Operations Planning, and marketing services manager. Figure 4.6 lists the primary responsibilities of a demand planner.

If you are just starting out to improve your company's forecasts, begin by asking about the origin of the current forecast or business plan numbers. Those numbers were generated through some sort of thought process. It may have been as simple as: we assume that the business this year will be about the same as last year and that the mix of products will be about the same. This assumption may be correct,

Figure 4.5

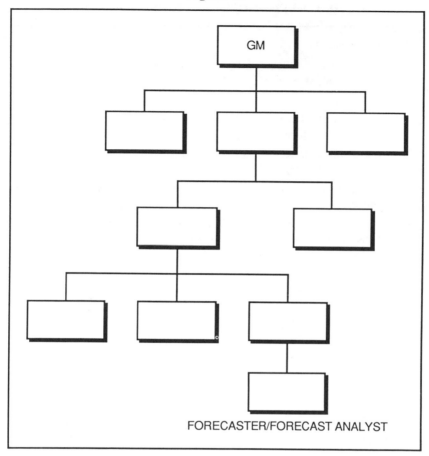

Caution: Do not place the forecasting function too low in the organization.

or it may prove to be inaccurate when looked at in more depth.

Let's explore this case a bit further. Perhaps your company had average sales last year, no new products were introduced, and no new customers were added. In developing the forecast, you make the following assumptions: (1) the available business from your customers is anticipated to be about the same: (2) you have no plans to increase sales coverage or launch any new promotions: (3) you haven't planned

Figure 4.6
Demand Planner/Manager Responsibilities

Primary Responsibility:

  Provide forecasts of anticipated demand to the company for Sales and Operations Planning and Master Production Scheduling.

Specific Responsibilities:

1. Develop forecasts of anticipated demand on a monthly basis by product family for Sales and Operations Planning.

2. Provide assistance to the sales organization facilitating the sales planning process for Sales and Operations Planning.

3. Provide product mix forecasts to the master scheduler for Master Production Scheduling.

4. Provide forecasts of anticipated demand for new products and/or new markets, working with product and marketing managers as appropriate.

5. Establish, maintain, and utilize forecasting and communications ''tools'' for accomplishing the above.

6. Assist in the development of marketing/manufacturing strategies, policies, and objectives including: the Sales and Operations Planning policy, the Master Production Scheduling policy, customer service objectives, inventory levels, backlog/lead time objectives, and planning time fences.

7. Assist with planning bills and product structures.

8. Monitor the company's performance to plan providing detailed input to sales and marketing management for use at the Sales and Operations Planning meetings.

9. Develop and document the factors and assumptions supporting the company sales plan.

Primary Qualifications:

1. Experience in sales, marketing, or customer service.

2. Knowledge of the company's products and services.

3. Knowledge of MRP II including Sales and Operations Planning, Master Production Scheduling, and demand management.

4. Excellent communications skills.

5. Credibility throughout the company; with top management, sales, manufacturing, engineering, finance and other support organizations.

6. Knowledge of the company's manufacturing processes.

7. Computer skills.

any changes in price: (4) you don't foresee any new competitors on the horizon. Considering these factors, the assumption that business will be about the same may be a reasonable one.

But let's say that the original forecast and sales plan were based on a certain assumption about the value of the dollar; that is, the dollar will remain at the same level as last year. The dollar suddenly rises, however, and international business takes a nosedive. If the performance of the dollar isn't monitored, your company will be operating under a false assumption, which could significantly impact the company's performance to the sales plan.

The fact is, for most companies the marketplace and internal operating conditions are changing continually. If you are going to improve forecasting, you constantly must make assumptions about the future on a wide variety of subjects, always observing the world inside and outside the company. You must also document, communicate, and monitor your major assumptions, so that when one or more of them changes, an informed adjustment can be made to the sales plan.

CROSS-TRAINING TO HELP GET STARTED

One of the biggest obstacles in getting a forecasting program started is understanding what each department needs in order to fulfill its responsibilities. The different departments, and people within those departments, can no longer operate alone. With demand planning, each is dependent upon the other for success in their jobs.

Early in our efforts at Bently Nevada, the marketing department's demand planners and manufacturing's production planners were continually at odds, and their conflicts were impeding the demand management process. In an attempt to develop a sense of teamwork, we set up a training experiment in which we physically moved the marketing people responsible for forecasting into the manufacturing planning area on a temporary basis. They attended manufacturing meetings, assisted in developing bill of material structure and revisions, and worked with the master scheduler on a daily basis to manage the Master Production Schedule. The forecasters also spent time on a "training desk" in the planning area.

The training desk program had been established to enable new planners to learn the system and become familiar with the manufacturing planning process. In addition, the marketing people responsible for forecasting consulted with the master scheduler and "booked" orders, made customer promises, rescheduled jobs in and out as necessary or as requested by sales, and generally became familiar with the overall system. Finally, they helped plan the manufacturing process, learned the problems associated with it, and became exposed to the decisions that planners must make on a daily basis.

In the end, we installed a "cross-training program" in which the manufacturing's master scheduler and marketing's demand planner switched jobs for six months. Co-author Joe Shull filled the position of master scheduler, taking total responsibility for executing the tasks of the position. At the same time, the master scheduler became the demand planner responsible for the forecasting function. This single step was probably the most significant in terms of creating a strong synergism and an environment of cooperation between marketing, sales, and manufacturing. Until that time, manufacturing's planning people had questioned the credibility of marketing's planning people in supplying information for the Manufacturing Resource Planning system, and vice versa. After this unique cross-training program, however, manufacturing's people saw that marketing in general, and the demand planner in particular, truly represented the customer. Also, as a result of this cross-training, the marketing organization gained real appreciation for the job of the master scheduler.

DEVELOPING A FORECAST

The challenge of demand planners is to make the best possible judgments about the future, based upon a wide range of information available. In addition to analyzing sales history, the following can help to improve your forecasts:

1. *Take advantage of other people's work.* Many other people and organizations are trying to predict the future. Numerous forecasts are available from a variety of sources. The federal government, for ex-

ample, collects, compiles, and publishes information that can be very helpful in providing information on economic trends and industry outlook. Business and trade periodicals are also a tremendous help. These sources of information not only provide historical information, but also often provide their own projections into the future. Customers are also a wealth of information—they're planning for their future business, and if you have a good relationship with them, they'll share their plans with you.

The direct linking of customers' plans to suppliers' plans is becoming increasingly common these days. We will discuss this more in the following chapter. Talk to your vendors, too. They may be serving mutual markets and have developed their own forecasts. And watch your competitors' news releases. Then listen for comments in the marketplace about the releases and how they are received.

2. *Monitor changes.* Carefully watch external factors that affect your business. Many companies can tie their bookings directly to external factors or events, such as interest rates, housing starts, or the price of oil. A demand planner should also carefully monitor internal factors, such as pricing plans, promotion plans, and new product introductions. Strive to determine which factors and plans most directly influence your booking levels. Use your personal computers to develop models, which incorporate those factors that have been shown to most directly affect your bookings.

3. *Continuously monitor your company's departmental plans.* They often have a way of coming true. Review your management reports. Monitor territory sales reports. Stay abreast of product plans and progress. Develop effective sales reporting techniques, including lost business, level of quote activity, and major project identification. Find out why you won or lost business. Remember, forecasting is a continuous activity, not a once a year event!

4. *Support the field salespeople.* The demand planner should assist the field salespeople in their sales planning efforts. He or she should provide feedback on the status of the sales plans and, in general, make it easy for the sales force to do sales planning.

5. *Group products into families.* In our discussion of Sales and Operations Planning, we explained the need to communicate in families. By grouping items into families, you will facilitate the forecasting pro-

cess, because it is easier to communicate and to manipulate the product mix forecast within product families. Also, when product families are structured to correspond roughly to market segments, measurement is more meaningful and changes are more easily implemented.

For example, let's say you manufacture items in a product family whose demand is dependent on levels of consumer credit. If available credit levels suddenly change, you should be able to interpret the impact on the aggregate sales plan for the appropriate product family. The shift in credit levels may affect some aggregate sales plans negatively, while other product family sales plans may be adjusted upward to reflect a positive impact on these market segments. The resulting change in the sales plan, of course, will be dependent on the development of modified sales strategies and the execution of sales tactics designed to redeploy the sales force.

6. *Participate in new product development.* A key demand management concept is to become involved in new product development early in the development cycle. When sales and marketing are involved early, they can help specify how the product is to be "packaged" and ordered by customers, which is part of the marketing/manufacturing strategic process in determining where a company will "meet its customers." This, in turn, allows greater communication between the demand planner and the sales force, ultimately resulting in more accurate sales plans.

7. *Adopt a "success" attitude.* At first, your forecasts may not be as accurate as you would like. This is only natural. If you document your assumptions and measure your performance, however, you're bound to improve. Firms that forecast well have developed measurement tools and an attitude that enables them to continually strive for improvement.

Part of developing a positive attitude about your forecast involves communicating with and seeking assistance from the people who must rely on the forecast. Build a teamwork environment with the users of your forecasts. With everyone participating, better understanding and a more positive attitude regarding forecasts will result.

FORECASTING TOOLS

Most people involved with forecasting or sales planning have their favorite method of analyzing historical data and projecting the numbers into the future. For some, it is three-month moving averages. For others, it is multiple regression analysis, exponential smoothing, least squares curve fitting, to name a few. Choosing the "proper" technique is a difficult and controversial task, and even when a consensus is reached, the market may change in ways that render the selected technique inappropriate. When this happens, changes in demand patterns may not be recognized until the technique is discovered to be no longer valid—a process that, by definition, occurs after the fact when it is too late to do anything about the situation.

Many statistical packages for personal computers are available to help reduce vast quantities of data and forecast more efficiently and effectively. It is important to provide your demand planners with tools that enable them to spend quality time analyzing the forecast data and communicating what the forecast information means, rather than just gathering the data. While we do not endorse any particular package, the Focus Forecasting approach is worth noting. Focus Forecasting was conceived and developed in 1972 by American Hardware Supply Company's Bernard T. Smith, who recognized the challenge of forecasting Thirty five thousand items for four thousand stores and six distribution centers. The company's twenty buyers were changing over 50 percent of the computer-generated forecasts. When asked why, the answers were all different, but sensible. The company's multitude of products, from light bulbs to snow shovels to lawn mowers, etc., all showed different demand patterns. Some items were new, others were being phased out. Some sold better in different geographical areas. Each buyer felt he knew more than the computer, and made his own adjustments. But the monthly forecasting cycle was just too time consuming.

Bernard Smith developed the Focus Forecasting technique based on the following premise: put all of the buyers' formulas into an automated system, pretend the last quarter hasn't yet happened, and let all the formulas forecast that quarter of known demand. Then measure which formula would have been most accurate in forecasting each item for the last quarter, and use that formula to forecast that item for the next quarter. In short, this technique allows the demand pattern inherent in the data to select the formula, rather than using a single formula to forecast all the data.

The strategies were easy to understand, so the user was comfortable with the results generated by the computer. Different strategies, or algorithms, could be chosen for different products that had different demand patterns.

Examples of the algorithms originally used in Focus Forecasting include:

1. Same as last year.
2. Seasonal like last year but 20 percent higher.
3. Last four months moving average.
4. Next three months will be half of last six months.
5. Last six months average minus 15 percent.
6. Twelve month moving average plus a 10 percent trend factor.
7. Forecast same as last year minus a 10 percent trend.
8. Override all of the above.

The Focus Forecasting approach allows the user to view historical data monthly or quarterly, and to view results in numerical or graphic format (see figure 4.7). One of the advantages of the Focus Forecasting method is that it looks for seasonality and trends. By looking at the data in several ways, the software can quickly find relationships and patterns that the demand planner might not otherwise see.

We know of hundreds of manufacturers and distributors that use the Focus Forecasting approach. We stress, however, that Focus Forecasting is not a foolproof way to generate a forecast for your firm. It only looks at history, and as with any historical forecast technique, it must be tempered with judgment and knowledge about the business and the marketplace.

COMMON FORECASTING PROBLEMS

A number of common problems are encountered when developing a forecast, many of which we learned the hard way. Usually, these prob-

Figure 4.7
Sample of Focus Forecasting Displays

PDue	83–84	84–85	85–86	86–87	System	Adj Fcst	MP	Sched
Jul		10141	6786	6616	9006			0
Aug		3972	4530	5569	5383			0
Sep		11162	8378	8596	10764			0
Oct		7353	6470	8831	8661			0
Nov		10243	8285	9257	10623			0
Dec		9552	5857	4395	7571			0
Jan		4597	2320	5882	6911			0
Feb	7263	3937	3347	4193	6197			0
Mar	4941	3799	3818	6031	7370			0
Apr	7577	5358	4659	5974	7575			0
May	7336	4755	7207	7709	9318			0
Jun	11979	6091	7216	9771	10933			0
Total		80960	68873	82824	100312			0
5th Q					29525			0

(Notes On File)

Item:	Model 100		Class: Portables	12 Mo Trend:	13951	20.3%
Desc:	Battery operated			On Hand:	3456	
Cost:		1.000	Price	2.000	Safety Stock:	3500
Form:	11	07/01	Error:	8.1	−3.8	Lead Time: 0 Days

F4 Other Prompts / A,B,C,DD,DI,DM,DT,E,F,F2,F10,G,Help,L,MA,MP,N,nn, i . .

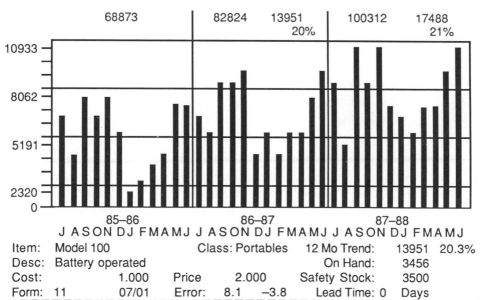

Item:	Model 100		Class: Portables	12 Mo Trend:	13951	20.3%
Desc:	Battery operated			On Hand:	3456	
Cost:		1.000	Price	2.000	Safety Stock:	3500
Form:	11	07/01	Error:	8.1	−3.8	Lead Time: 0 Days

(G) raph Annually / (R) oll Back / i History Screen . .

Sample of Focus Forecasting displays.
The upper display shows the history of this item and the forecast generated by the Focus Forecasting approach. The second display shows two years of history plus the forecast in graphic mode. (Courtesy of Decision Technologies, Inc.)

lems are the result of a misunderstanding of the forecasting process. Let's explore some of these problems.

- *Forecasts are biased.* If actual demand comes in consistently higher or lower than the forecast, you know that there is a bias somewhere in the forecast. Exuberant managers, for example, will tend to bias forecasts so that they are consistently higher than actual demand. These managers worry about product availability and the resultant lost business. Or, they believe that forecasting is a self-fulfilling prophecy, and that within reason the firm will sell to any forecast level. So why not aim high? In contrast, pessimistic managers will tend to influence forecasts downward, so that they are consistently lower than actual demand. These managers worry about inventory levels affecting "bottom line" performance, or they may be concerned about the business outlook. After all, the only penalty is a little longer lead time, so why not be conservative on your forecasts?

  Forecasts may also be biased towards favored product lines at the expense of others because of management loyalty, profitability, or fear of change. Sometimes forecasts are intentionally low simply to allow the organization to look good when the projections are exceeded.

  Forecasts from the sales organization may be biased if the forecasts are linked to incentive and quota programs. It is natural for a salesman to provide a low forecast if he is to be rewarded for how much he sells above it. Product managers will sometimes bias a forecast by projecting unrealistic sales volumes to ensure product introduction budgets.

- *Forecasts are ignored.* One problem with forecasts is that time and energy are often spent to develop them, but they are then ignored by the people who are supposed to use them. This typically happens if the forecasts are considered unreliable by the users. When this occurs, the demand planner needs to improve communications with the users to understand why they consider them to be unreliable. Efforts must then be made by the demand planner to improve the forecast reliability and gain the confidence of the users.

- *There are no incentives for reliable forecasting.* In many companies, "forecast" is a four-letter word. Not surprisingly, we rarely see a company where there are incentives or rewards for reliable forecasting—forecasts are only talked about when they're wrong. When was the last time anyone in your company praised the forecaster or demand planner for doing a good job? Unfortunately, without incentives and positive reinforcement, improvement rarely occurs.

- *Forecasts are generated at the wrong level.* Often, companies forecast at a level that is not optimal for achieving accuracy. The cure may lie in reviewing what they're forecasting. For example, by forecasting at a semi-finished level instead of at a finished goods level, improvements in forecasting accuracy may result. Specific combinations of product options may be impossible to forecast accurately. Companies sometimes forecast at too detailed a level, making the job harder than it needs to be for the demand planner. At the opposite end of the spectrum, some companies forecast without sufficient detail to be used by manufacturing in their production planning process. The bottom line is that there's an optimum level at which the product demands can best be forecast.

- *There's no accountability for forecasting.* Who is accountable for the forecast? The demand planner? Sales? Marketing? Management? Manufacturing? Initially, the forecast of anticipated demand needs to be developed by someone who accepts responsibility and accountability for the task. This person is usually the forecaster or demand planner. One of the points we are hoping to make in this book is that to gain a competitive edge, *all* of the departments and *all* of the organizations in the company need to work together as a team. Once the forecast has become the company sales plan, all departments work together to turn that plan into reality.

- *Forecast methodology is not well understood.* The field of forecasting is replete with statistical techniques used to tie historical data bases to external and internal indicators. These techniques and their application can be intimidating to the uninitiated. As a result, many firms fail to understand the proper application of forecasting methods and, as a result, do not achieve satisfactory results.

Throughout this chapter, we have discussed the development of forecasts, warning of problems that you will likely encounter. In the next chapter, we'll describe how to gain the commitment from your selling organization to turn a forecast into a sales plan. We'll also discuss how to ensure that there is support from sales to sell the plan.

CHECKLIST

1. Are the forecast users' needs clearly understood?
2. Do the forecast users truly rely upon the forecast, or is the forecast "second-guessed"?
3. Does the forecasting process include taking "different views of the elephant"?
4. Is there a formal process of documenting the assumptions behind the forecast?
5. Are all demand streams included in the forecasting process?
6. Are all available inputs used by the demand planner in developing the forecast?
7. Is there clear responsibility and accountability for the development and maintenance of the forecast?
8. Does the demand planning function use available computerized tools to assist in the forecasting effort?
9. Is the demand planner aware of and watchful for common forecasting problems, such as bias in the forecast?

Chapter 5

Building Effective Sales Plans

Ladies and gentlemen, that young man knows the difference between c'mere *and* sic 'em.

—**Frank Broyles**

The Difference Between a Sales Plan and a Forecast

Many people assume that a sales plan and a forecast of anticipated demand are one and the same. But they are often very different projections, and must be treated as such. The fundamental difference between the two is aptly illustrated by an event that took place during a football game between Georgia Tech and Notre Dame. Frank Broyles, former head coach at the University of Arkansas, was the commentator for the nationally televised NCAA game. Georgia Tech had a small but speedy defensive back, and Notre Dame, as usual, had a large, strong fullback. On one play, Notre Dame had the ball, hiked it, and handed it off to the fullback, who was immediately tackled five yards behind the line of scrimmage by the much smaller Georgia Tech defensive back. Frank Broyles, in his own southern way, said, "Now ladies and gentlemen, that young man knows the difference between *c'mere* and *sic 'em.*"

How does this relate to forecasting of anticipated demand and sales planning? Forecasting is "c'mere"—if the numbers are achieved, it's often by accident. Sales planning, on the other hand, implies a commitment to sell the game plan. In other words, it's "sic 'em"—which

89

is exactly what happens when a fired-up sales force agrees to hit the company's target goals.

In more concrete terms, a forecast of anticipated demand is an estimate or prediction of what customers will ask you to deliver during your planning horizon and is based on a review of history, external and internal indicators, market segment conditions, promotional strategies, pricing considerations, and documentation of assumptions made about the future of the company's marketplace. It is normally communicated in the Sales and Operations Planning process by product line.

In contrast, a sales plan is what the sales organization has committed to sell. It is supported by individual sales objectives, customer and territory plans, market channel plans, and product plans. It is usually stated by customer or territory, with target accounts and action plans formulated to reach the sales objectives.

Forecasts can be turned into sales plans, however, when:

1. They are agreed to by sales, marketing, and management.
2. Sales has made a commitment to sell the plan, to make it happen.
3. Accountability is accepted by sales.
4. The sales plans are supported by all organizations of the company.

All companies engage in some kind of sales planning, and many do it well. But the companies that are proficient at sales planning are most often the ones that need to improve the communication links between the marketplace and their factory. For example, one of the companies with which we're familiar is encountering tremendous sales growth through increased market penetration and the development of new markets. The sales organization is extremely well managed, with sales plans by individual salespeople. Sales objectives have been established by customer and product line, and performance is measured both in aggregate and detail on a monthly basis. The factors affecting sales are reviewed and documented, with contingency plans made in anticipation of changes to those factors in the future.

Though this sales organization is very successfully increasing bookings, the manufacturing organization is struggling to meet the increased demand. There is no formal communication mechanism in place for manufacturing to take advantage of the excellent sales planning being done in the company. In this case, the implementation of a formalized MRP II program is being sponsored by the sales and marketing organization to provide the formal mechanism for communicating plans and linking the sales plan to the manufacturing plan. If you find yourself in a similar situation, take heart; there is a solution, if you will take the lead.

While we do not presume to know your customers or markets, we believe we can help sales get better support from manufacturing by showing how to develop plans that are not only useful for managing sales, but can also be used in Manufacturing Resource Planning.

ABOUT BOTTOM-UP SALES PLANNING

A sales plan includes what the company expects to sell and the detailed actions required for success. It is based on customer plans and the sales organization's knowledge of those plans. Sales history by customer is used as a reference to start the sales planning process. The responsible salesperson normally develops a set of objectives for each of his or her key accounts based on current customer problems and opportunities, inventory levels, and budgets. Those objectives are then supported by an action plan that may include the number and type of sales calls, demonstrations to key people, customer seminars, and/or other promotional activities. When this process is completed, the salesperson has a customer account plan. The summary of all customer account plans is the foundation of the bottom-up sales plan. This plan will be reviewed, negotiated, and adjusted through the sales management process using top-down sales goals.

To help make the sales plan usable by manufacturing and other company support organizations, the customer account plan should have sales by product line. The expected sales can be expressed in units, but are most often expressed in dollars. For best communications, it should be expressed in both dollars *and* units. If it is communicated in dollars, it must be translatable into units.

A key way to improve the usefulness of the sales planning information for the company is to include not only the timing of bookings (sales by expected date of order receipt), but the anticipated delivery requirements of the customer (customer need date) as well. This way, the information on timing not only assists in sales management, but also provides a forecast of anticipated demand, which can be used by the rest of the company.

In most cases, the planning horizon for the sales force should be the same as the planning horizon for Sales and Operations Planning. The plans of individual salespeople should be updated regularly, depending on the volatility of the markets your company serves. Monthly updates by the individual salespeople are desirable. If customer demand is changing rapidly, you also may want to temporarily update the plans more frequently until the fluctuations in demand return to a more predictable level. As you refine your abilities to monitor the marketplace, you will determine when updates are required to reflect accurately changes in demand. In any case, bear in mind that sales management will be asked to agree to changes to the sales plan at the Sales and Operations Planning meeting, which is most often held on a monthly basis.

TIPS FOR BOTTOM-UP SALES PLANNING

When developing a sales plan that can be used in a Manufacturing Resource Planning system, several factors should be considered. First, there's the issue of timing and time fences; sales needs to understand the concept of time fences, as discussed earlier. As we described, there is a point in time at which changes in manufacturing are difficult and costly to make. Sales should use its knowledge of these fences to properly manage fluctuations in demand by negotiating product availability/delivery dates with customers. Time fences or windows are not inviolate, however, and sales can use its understanding of manufacturing to negotiate changes in the production plan. Since sales is closest to the marketplace, it not only must represent the company to the customer, but the customer to the company as well. That means sales has the responsibility of communicating to other organizations when changes in time fences or windows are necessary to meet customer needs.

Another factor in developing a sales plan effective enough for manufacturing to use is the level of detail. Usually, sales (expressed in dollars and units) by major product lines are adequate for the sales planning process. But many firms, particularly those that sell large, expensive products with costly or long lead time options, may require additional detail input on product or option mix from the sales force.

In any case, the sales plan should include enough detail to allow effective use of the plan. At the same time, you don't want to bog down your sales force with undue administrative burdens. Despite its importance, sales planning is, after all, a non-selling activity, and the old maxim "Keep your salespeople's feet on the street" applies today more than ever. For this reason one of the demand planner's functions is to facilitate the sales planning process. The demand planner should provide administrative support in the collection of data, the analysis of data, and the communication of detailed sales forecasts to manufacturing. Often, the most productive way to assist sales in its sales planning is to provide it with a forecast that it can then change, instead of asking it to start with a blank piece of paper. When this approach is used, a "silence is approval" rule should be invoked.

One final factor that needs to be considered for sales planning to be of use in Manufacturing Resource Planning is timeliness of input. The time required to develop and communicate changes to the sales plan, gain approval, and implement those changes through Sales and Operations Planning and the Master Production Schedule can be significant in some firms. Sales must strive to reduce the time required to communicate changes so that manufacturing has as much time as possible to respond to changes in demand as communicated by the sales organization.

When we initially began to use sales planning as part of the demand planning process at Bently Nevada, the time from starting the process until manufacturing received our inputs was approximately three weeks. Since our Sales and Operations Planning process was on a monthly schedule, this allowed little time for manufacturing to prepare for the session. We attacked the problem and reduced the preparation time to less than one week.

We're familiar with a company in the Southwest where it takes sales and marketing six weeks to provide their input to manufacturing. Yet, the company updates its plans on a monthly basis. Consequently, the value of sales' and marketing's input is certainly questionable. In some situations, sales and marketing know the aggregate sales information before they know the detail product mix. In these cases, it is helpful to manufacturing for sales and marketing to communicate the aggregate information as soon as it is known, then later follow up with information on detail product mix.

One final point with regard to bottom-up sales planning needs to be made: documenting the assumptions on which the sales plan is based and making contingency plans are as important during the sales planning process as they are during the Sales and Operations Planning and the forecasting processes. The principles described in earlier chapters on documenting assumptions and contingency, or "what if?" planning, directly apply to sales planning.

THOUGHTS BEHIND SALES PLANNING

We have found that companies with effective sales planning processes take into account the following kinds of questions when developing their sales plans:

- *Customers*. What is the financial condition of your major customers? What is the condition of the market on which they depend for their livelihood? What are their plans and objectives? Is your product in their budget? Are you getting all their business? Are you increasing your share? Are you making products your customers want to buy?

- *New products*. What new products are you planning to introduce in the next year? How will they affect your sales plan? How will they affect existing products? Will they make you more competitive? Are you likely to win orders you might not otherwise have received? Will the new products displace current products, and should you be planning accordingly?

- *Competition*. How healthy are your competitors? Are they adding sales coverage? How effective is their sales force? How are they viewed by your customers? Are you likely to win business from them? If so, what products will be affected? How do you compete on price, quality, and service?

- *Distribution inventory.* What are the levels of inventories of your distributors? What are their inventory goals? What is their financial condition? What is their competitive environment? What is the condition of the market on which they depend for their livelihood? Are they expanding their coverage? What are your distribution plans? Are you adding coverage?

- *Bidding activity.* What is the level of outstanding quotes? What major projects are you planning to bid on? What are the probabilities of winning? What are the probabilities that the projects will be let? Who are you competing against? What product are you competing against? If you win the bid, what other follow-on products will you likely book?

  Many companies are fortunate in that a large percentage of their business is quoted prior to receiving customer orders. In these situations, it is desirable to input the quotations into a personal computer and use this information in developing a forecast of anticipated demand. A well-designed system allows for the forecast to be presented in a variety of ways—by customer, territory, salesman, and product. These presentations should be *time phased* by customer delivery date and should allow for factoring the probability of receiving an order.

- *Economic factors.* What are the major factors affecting business with your customers? Are they trending up or down? If they are trending down, what customers may benefit by an inverse relationship?

- *Pricing strategy.* What are the firm's plans for price adjustments? Is the discount policy changing? What are your competitors' pricing tendencies? How will this affect your sales?

- *Market analysis.* How strong are your markets? What is the outlook for them? What economic and political factors affect their health and well-being? Can you project a trend?

- *Technology.* Will new technology affect your selling tactics? What product lines and markets are affected? How are competitive products affected?

- *Corporate management strategy.* What is your corporate strategy for market share and growth? How may this strategy affect your overall bookings? How may it affect bookings by product line? What engineering and service support functions are expected to boost bookings? What planned new product and sales training programs will help boost bookings, and by how much? What promotional efforts are planned? How will these affect your bookings? How will changes in the incentive program affect bookings?

- *Historical sales data.* Do you have a good customer data base? Is it relevant to future business? What has been the traditional mix of product lines and options? What is the trend? What seasonality exists in the bookings figures? Can you expect the trend to continue? Is the historical mix of customers and projects roughly the same, or have there been major changes or shifts in your marketplace? How will these changes affect bookings?

- *Contingency, or "What if?" planning.* What external market, economic, or political factors could affect the business? Will plans need to be adjusted up or down if one of these factors changes? Is the sales force prepared with contingency plans to sell the company sales plan even under adverse conditions? What alternative sales strategies, tactics, and programs could be employed to avoid adjusting the company's sales plan downward?

- *Assumptions.* Are the assumptions for each item outlined above documented? Are these assumptions based on solid, factual information, or are they artificially derived by a subjective financial figure or biased input?

SERVICE AND REPAIR PARTS

If service and repair parts are a significant portion of your company's business, they should be considered in your sales plan. Service demand is often overlooked by firms in the sales planning process, because people in the sales organization often feel little responsibility for selling spare parts. Even though the orders may trickle in on their own, they still represent a demand on the factory and must be included in resource planning.

Many companies acknowledge that their spare parts business is a key contributor to the "bottom line," yet marketing, sales, and management of this portion of the total business take a back seat to sales of new equipment. As a result, spare parts frequently are not included in the sales planning process. This has two effects. First, opportunities for sales of profitable spare parts are often missed. Second, when significant spare-parts business is received, it shows up as a surprise since it was not included in the company sales plan. As a result, manufacturing may have difficulty in meeting requested customer delivery dates.

A number of the major capital equipment manufacturers view spare parts as a separate category and treat them with the same importance as major product lines. This approach helps to ensure that spare parts are considered from a sales and marketing point of view, and that materials and capacity are planned for their sale.

MEASURING YOUR SALES PLAN

It is crucial to continually measure actual demand against the sales plan as it is booked. This is necessary to monitor sales performance as well as to improve the communications and demand planning process. Feedback should be supplied periodically to all members of the sales force, advising them of their actual orders versus the anticipated orders in the sales plans. Updates to the plan should be required from the salespeople even if their recommendation is "no change." If adjustments to the sales plan are to be made, there should be a full understanding of:

1. Why the adjustment is necessary, and
2. What assumptions are incorrect or are no longer valid.

As we gain exposure to more and more companies, we find there are two distinct categories of sales organizations. The first is one that plans its sales and subsequently sells the plan (see figure 5.1). The second is one that operates more in a reactive, order taking mode.

Figure 5.1

"Nice try, Murdock. But the only way to raise the sales figures is to *sell.*"

Reprinted by permission of Sales and Marketing Magazine,
copyright (September 1986)

Companies with sales organizations that function as order takers are often young, high growth companies in which the business is driven largely through its product superiority. Usually, the product services a new need and/or is technically superior to others on the market. Few companies can afford this luxury for long. As the product matures, competition or growth objectives of the company forces the sales organization to plan its sales and aggressively sell the plan.

It is important to strive continually to improve sales planning performance, no matter how accurate your plans seem to be. Sales planning performance, when the program begins, will naturally be less accurate than desired. Don't despair, though; with experience, measurement, and feedback, your performance is sure to improve. The process will not only help boost sales plan accuracy, but it will also enhance the effectiveness of your overall sales effort. The "high bar" must be raised continually in today's competitive environment in order to maintain, or gain, market position.

CUSTOMER LINKING

As more companies implement MRP II/JIT/TQC, there has been a movement toward direct linking between customers and manufacturers. Companies that link successfully with the customers get so close to their customers that their customers' plans become part of their plans. Walt Goddard, of The Oliver Wight Companies, describes customer linking as "eliminating the need for forecasting." In essence, he is saying that you are letting your customers forecast for you.

Manufacturers have been linking with their suppliers since the late 1970s through an approach called "vendor scheduling." With vendor scheduling, the purchaser eliminates the use of traditional purchase orders and communicates through vendor schedules instead. This linking with suppliers through vendor scheduling should not be confused with receiving a blanket order with release dates. Whereas vendor scheduling implies a blanket contract, a bilateral agreement, its most significant characteristic is frequent communications between customer and supplier of time-phased future requirements. The customer shares his plans from his MRP II system with his vendors on a regular basis, often weekly.

Vendor scheduling provides the supplier with visibility of demand over a planning horizon and indicates authorization for the supplier to ship product. In essence, the purchaser is sharing his schedules and forecasts with his supplier. Some of the benefits of this approach to the purchaser are: (1) lower inventories (they get what they need just when they need it), (2) lower prices through volume purchasing, (3) shorter lead times, (4) less paperwork, and (5) a more reliable and committed supplier.

Benefits of vendor scheduling to the supplier include: (1) the booking of all, or most, of the customer's available business; (2) visibility of the customer's schedules and forecasts, enabling manufacturing and purchasing to plan and schedule more productively; (3) less direct selling time; and (4) less paperwork. We highly recommend that sales and marketing people read *High Performance Purchasing*, by John E. Schorr and Thomas F. Wallace. This book describes the use of vendor schedules and will help sales and marketing to understand what their traditional "adversary"—purchasing—is being taught in companies operating with an MRP II operating system.

Some firms are linked directly via computer through Electronic Data Interchange (EDI), enabling customers to check availability and to place orders directly with suppliers. Customer linking not only helps to improve planning and scheduling for both parties, but it almost always ensures that the supplier gets a larger share of a customer's business. Linking promotes more teamwork between customers and suppliers. The teamwork leads to reduced costs and stronger bonds that are difficult for competitors to overcome, giving the supplier an even more formidable marketing edge.

The 3M Company, for example, successfully uses customer linking to improve its service. Adversely affected by erratic demand from several large-volume customers, 3M reasoned that customer linking was a way of reducing the uncertainty of this demand. 3M based its customer linking program on the premise, "It's the customer that creates the demand for the plan and by so doing, controls to various degrees what is produced and how often", according to Steven N. Burns of 3M. So, 3M went directly to the source of the demand—the customer—and developed a program that allowed the customer to predict the demand.

Steven N. Burns, in a paper presented at the APICS International Conference in 1987, described the following benefits 3M received from its customer linking program:

- Reduced fluctuations in demand.
- One hundred percent on-time deliveries, which enabled 3M to achieve certified vendor status with customers participating in the program.
- Facilitation of its JIT program "It would have been difficult at best to implement JIT within the plant without addressing the fluctuations in demand first," Burns states (see figures 5.2 and 5.3).

By linking with large-volume customers, 3M improved communications between the company and its customers. Improved communications enabled 3M to utilize its customers' plans to move away from

Figure 5.2
Customer Demand History
3M

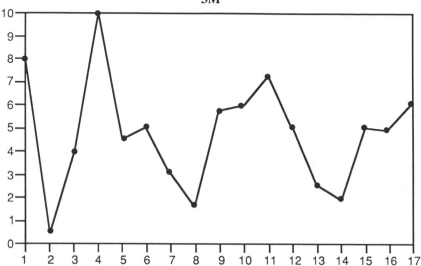

Customer demand prior to customer linking was erratic and unpredictable.

supplying large lot sizes to supplying products based upon the flow of demand, which is a natural outgrowth of JIT/TQC efforts.

While there are many advantages to customer linking, it should not be pursued blindly, as it poses problems if improperly implemented. These problems can include requests for lower pricing in return for increased volume and scheduling problems caused by inconsistent customer demand coupled with a lack of agreement with customers on time fences, leading to customer dissatisfaction. These problems, however, can be avoided with awareness, preparation, and proper customer communication, education, and negotiation. In an attempt to create this link, we have seen some companies jointly send purchasing people from the customer's company and marketing people from the supplier's company to the Oliver Wight MRP II class for purchasing. They use the class as a stimulus to negotiate the agreement defining the new customer-vendor relationship.

Though the benefits of customer linking seem fairly obvious, the

Figure 5.3

Customer Demand History
3M

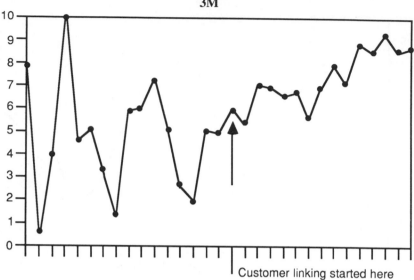

Customer linking started here

Reductions in fluctuations and uncertainty resulted after customer linking.

sales force must be educated to understand the advantages of direct linking. In some cases, linking may be a culture shock for a salesperson who believes that he or she must personally handle every customer order and communication. With linking, the salesperson is bypassed during routine scheduling, and the companies' planners communicate directly with the customers, which can leave some salespeople feeling a loss of account control. This concern is overcome when the sales force understands the concept and sees the benefits of customer linking.

In actuality, in addition to creating a barrier to competitors, customer linking frees a salesperson from the drudgery of routine purchase order paperwork so that he or she has more time to book incremental business. In other words, when customer linking is properly implemented, it's a win-win-win situation.

TEAMWORK AND COOPERATION FOR SUCCESS

If your company has a direct link between those who are responsible for forecasting and those who are responsible for sales, better sales plans and better forecasts are inevitable. As sales plans change—and they inevitably will—the demand planner simply includes the change in the forecast. To facilitate this effort, the sales organization must keep the demand planner appraised of customer plans, competitive shifts, incentive programs, and anything else that may influence demand forecasts and underlying business assumptions.

The major benefit of "the assumption-consensus approach to forecasting" is that the resulting sales plans really *do* become self-fulfilling prophecies. When the sales plans are agreed to by the people who have to execute them, they have a remarkable tendency to become real. In short, if you want improved forecast accuracy, change your forecasts into sales plans with the entire company working as a team to support them.

CHECKLIST

1. Is your sales planning oriented around a "sic 'em" attitude; that is, do you have a commitment from the sales force to sell the company's sales plan?
2. Does your sales plan include what the company expects to sell and the detailed actions required for success over a planning horizon?
3. Do your sales people develop a set of sales objectives for each of their key accounts, based on current customer problems and opportunities, inventory levels, and budgets? Are those objectives supported by an action plan?
4. Is the sales force's "bottom-up" sales plan reviewed, negotiated, and through the sales management process, using top-down sales goals, derived from the demand planning process?

5. Is the sales plan expressed by customer and product line? Are timing of bookings and anticipated customer delivery requirements included in the sales plan?

6. Are the individual salespeople's plans updated regularly?

7. When developing a sales plan that can be used by manufacturing, does the sales force consider timing and time fences? Is the sales plan communicated in the amount of detail required by manufacturing for production planning, preferably in units and dollars?

8. Is "what if?" sales planning performed? Are contingency plans made for factors that may change unexpectedly?

9. Is the actual demand as it is booked continually measured against the sales plan? Is feedback supplied regularly to all members of the sales force, advising them of their actual orders versus their sales plans?

10. Are the assumptions behind the sales plan documented?

11. When sales plans change, does the demand planner include the change in the forecast?

12. Are you actively pursuing customer linking?

Chapter 6

Turning Plans into Reality: The Master Production Schedule

Take care to get what you like, or you will be forced to like what you get.
—**George Bernard Shaw**

"Why should I worry about how the Master Production Schedule is developed or what goes in it?" asked a marketing manager at a firm that was implementing MRP II. "All the MPS does is tell manufacturing what to build."

His view is a common one. The importance of the Master Production Schedule (MPS) in successfully executing demand strategies is often overlooked, primarily because sales and marketing people don't realize its value in turning demand plans into reality. They view the Master Production Schedule solely as a concern of manufacturing. When considered from another perspective, however, the value of the MPS to sales and marketing soon becomes apparent; if the Master Production Schedule determines what manufacturing is going to build, then it also determines what products will be available to sell and when. This information can be very valuable for salespeople when negotiating with customers.

This chapter discusses how the MPS can be used to improve product availability and customer promising. It also explores policy issues that sales and marketing can influence when developing a Master Production Schedule as part of an MRP II implementation project, which will ensure improved customer service performance. These policy issues

105

include mechanisms for handling order promising, order entry, and abnormal demand.

WHAT IS A MASTER PRODUCTION SCHEDULE?

To understand how the MPS turns plans into reality, you must first understand the role of the MPS in the sales and production process. Companies that use MRP II view the Master Production Schedule as a link between sales and marketing and manufacturing, just as Sales and Operations Planning links those groups. But whereas Sales and Operations Planning links sales and marketing and manufacturing at the management level, the MPS provides the link at the detail level (see figure 6.1). In providing this connection, the MPS uses the production plan that results from the Sales and Operations Planning process, along with the detailed mix forecast supplied by sales and marketing, to determine what products the company will build and when it will build them.

In essence, the function of the MPS is to balance supply and demand on a detail or item level, day to day, week to week, as shown in figure 6.2. The American Production and Inventory Control Society (APICS) defines the MPS as

> . . . a statement of what the company expects to manufacture. It is the anticipated build schedule for those selected items assigned to the Master Scheduler.
>
> The Master Scheduler maintains this schedule and, in turn, it becomes a set of planning numbers which drives MRP. It represents what the company plans to produce, expressed in specific configurations, quantities, and dates.
>
> The MPS should not be confused with a sales forecast, which represents a statement of demand. The MPS must take the forecast, plus other important considerations (backlog, availability of material and capacity, management policy and goals, etc.) into account prior to determining the best manufacturing strategy.

In balancing supply and demand on a detail level, the Master Production Schedule has five primary goals:

Figure 6.1

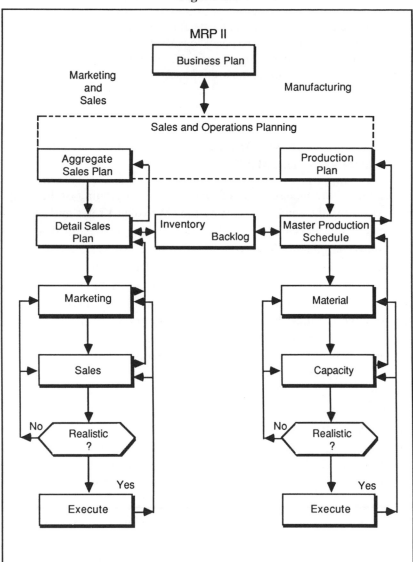

The closed loop MRP II process.

1. Execute the production plan as determined in Sales and Operations Planning.
2. Support customer orders and the detailed mix forecast.
3. Regulate the company's response to market demand.
4. Manage the manufacturing resources of the firm.
5. Balance the firm's needs versus its capabilities.

WHY SHOULD SALES AND MARKETING CONTRIBUTE TO THE DEVELOPMENT OF THE MPS?

The marketing manager we referenced at the beginning of this chapter was asking the same thing. Why me? Why can't sales and marketing let the master scheduler and manufacturing managers determine what they want the MPS to do in implementing MRP II?

The answer is simple. Because the MPS determines what products will be available, it is the basis for making (and keeping) promises to customers. In making promises that satisfy customers' expectations, a broad viewpoint must be considered. It is not enough to observe only from manufacturing's perspective. While manufacturing needs the MPS to provide scheduling stability for meeting promised dates and producing higher quality products at lower manufacturing costs, sales and marketing need the MPS to link their sales plans and forecasts to the manufacturing execution system. The MPS provides sales and marketing the means for communicating their plans to manufacturing, so that manufacturing can execute according to the sales plan. Further, the Master Production Schedule allows sales to know what manufacturing is planning to build and, therefore, what is available for sale. The MPS functions of an MRP II system enable MRP II to become a *company* system, rather than just a *manufacturing* system. It is thus the link between planning and execution.

For sales and marketing to ensure that the Master Production Schedule fulfills these needs, they must be involved in the development of MPS policies during the implementation stage of an MRP II project. Sales and marketing managers, the master scheduler, manufacturing managers, and company management jointly determine at this time how the following issues will be handled:

1. How will delivery dates for customer orders be promised? By whom? ("Customer orders" include interplant demand, international demand, distribution demand, and demands from all other demand streams.)

2. What time fences will be used? (This question is of primary importance in ensuring the stability of manufacturing schedules.)

3. What authority will allow change within time fences? (The MPS policy must include the ability to handle emergency or opportunity orders—with appropriate visibility to management.)

4. Under what authority will changes in customer priorities be made? (Someone within the organization needs to be responsible for establishing the priority of customer orders on a continuous basis.)

5. What specifically should be included in the Master Production Schedule? Should end items be included, or is there some alternative approach that would simplify the scheduling task and provide more flexibility to the marketplace?

6. Who will be responsible for providing the detailed forecast to the master scheduler? Will a demand manager function be established?

7. How will performance to the Master Production Schedule be measured? Who is accountable for meeting the objectives of the aggregate production plan?

AVAILABLE-TO-PROMISE/AVAILABLE-TO-SELL

One of the most common complaints from salespeople, particularly in make-to-order manufacturing companies, is their firms' inability to meet customer delivery dates or the failure to have product available when the customer requests it. Many companies are overcoming these problems through the use of the available-to-promise (ATP) function in the MPS system. The ATP function indicates the number of units in inventory or in the Master Production Schedule that have not been committed to customer orders. It tells how much product is still available-to-promise to customers, and in what time frame, as described in the following January, 1980 *Report* by Richard C. Ling:

> ATP information is deceptively simple to put together. For many businesses, it's a matter of comparing time-phased customer commitments

Figure 6.2

Stocked Item	1	2	3	4	5	6	7	8
Forecast								
Production Forecast								
Actual Demand			12		7		2	
Projected Available Balance	15							
Available-to-Promise		3			16			25
MPS					25			25

An example of a cumulative ATP of three in weeks one to three, 19 in weeks four to seven, and 44 in week eight.

to the on-hand balance plus the Master Production Schedule. (Figures 6.2 and 6.3 illustrate ATP calculations.)

ATP is calculated by comparing the actual demand to the on-hand and MPS receipts over time. Twelve units are committed to customers in week two. Since the 25 units due in week four are coming too late to cover this commitment, 12 of the 15 on-hand must be reserved to meet it; thus three are available-to-promise in the current week.

In a similar manner, nine of the 25 due in week four are reserved to meet customer commitments of seven in week four and two in week six. Thus, 16 of the 25 are available-to-promise. The 25 due in week eight are all available-to-promise since there are no customer demands presently against that receipt. Note that the latest available receipt is used to satisfy a given customer commitment.

Some firms prefer a cumulative display of ATP. In that case, in figure 6.2, the cumulative ATP would be three in weeks one to three, 19 in weeks four to seven, and 44 in week eight.

Figure 6.3 illustrates the one tricky aspect of ATP logic. Proceeding as in Figure 6.2, one would originally expect to see an ATP of three in week one. However, a total of 27 actual customer orders exist in weeks four and six for the 25 due in week four. This creates a negative ATP

Figure 6.3

Stocked Item	1	2	3	4	5	6	7	8
Forecast								
Production Forecast								
Actual Demand		12		14		13		
Projected Available Balance	15							
Available-to-Promise		1		0				25
MPS				25				25

An illustration of one tricky aspect of ATP logic. The standard logic handles a negative ATP of minus two by reaching back for the earlier ATP, which reduces the original three to one in week one.

of minus two, which the standard logic handles by reaching back for earlier ATP. This reach back reduces the original three to one in week one.

In many businesses, capacity, not materials, is the driver for available-to-promise. Many capacity-managed businesses, such as foundries, contract machining operations, plastics molding, textiles process and engineer-to-order businesses, fit this mold. In these businesses, customer promises are primarily based on capacity availability, not material availability. Either rough-cut capacity profiles or estimating processes are used to convert incoming customer orders to demands on critical capacities, such as people, facilities, engineering functions, etc. These demands are then used to make "available-to-promise" capacity commitments.

Figure 6.4 illustrates the ATP capacity process for a bank of injection molding machines.

The ATP mechanism keeps track of all existing commitments. It ensures that we account for all existing commitments against our capabilities so that we don't over-promise these resources. Many manufacturing companies have developed responsive, available-to-promise processes.

Figure 6.4

Capacity Booking

	1	2	3	4	5	6
Molding Hours	240	240	240	280	280	280
Sold	240	240	180	140	70	
Available-to-Promise	0	0	60	140	210	280

An illustration of the ATP capacity process for a bank of injection molding machines.

Many commercial software packages now have these capabilities as a fairly standard feature.

When sales and marketing people have access to ATP information and receive training to understand the significance of the numbers in the ATP, they can use this information as a competitive weapon. The ATP information enables sales and marketing personnel to make decisions that support their customer plans and strategies while getting the maximum capacity from the manufacturing organization.

Consider, for example, a manufacturer of circuit boards in the San Francisco Bay area. This company was having problems with its customer service. After analyzing its situation, the company found it had sufficient capacity and materials in total throughout the year to meet demand, but the timing of customer orders was such that it was constantly making late shipments. When the company installed a Master Production Schedule with an ATP function, it gained the ability to see *what* products manufacturing was going to build and *when* it planned to build them. The manufacturer used this information to promise deliveries instead of making promises based on ''standard lead times.'' The result? Their customer service improved dramatically.

In addition to using available-to-promise to support customer plans and strategies, the ATP function also warns the sales and marketing organizations when product is not available and stimulates discussion and action for meeting customer demand. For example, a sales manager for a hardware manufacturer was reluctant to use the ATP function when it was initially installed, fearing it would put an unnecessary constraint on the sales department. He began to see the value of the ATP function, however, when the customer service organization started using it to make customer delivery promises. As a result, he became a true believer in the ATP function the day a customer service representative notified him that they were about to begin promising longer than normal lead times to customers. The advance warning enabled the sales manager to work with manufacturing in adjusting their manufacturing plans to reduce lead times to a level that better satisfied customer expectations. "Before we had ATP, I found out about delivery lead time problems after the fact—when products began shipping late. Now, we can work out problems in advance," the sales manager told us.

WHAT MAKES A GOOD PROMISE?

When salespeople complain about their company's inability to meet customer delivery dates, they generally blame manufacturing for causing delivery problems. And manufacturing generally faults sales and marketing for making promises that can't be kept.

Analysis has shown, however, that the root cause of the problem is often the use of two independent systems. We find that the manufacturing system and the sales system are often developed independently and are not designed to be linked together. As a result, sales often makes delivery promises based on "standard lead times," without regard for what is in inventory or what has been scheduled to be produced.

Faced with the same situation, a manufacturer of office equipment in the Midwest used the MPS portion of its MRP II system with an ATP function to link together the forecasting and order entry systems employed by sales and marketing and manufacturing. This link gave sales the information describing what was available to sell and when it was available-to-promise. It also gave manufacturing the visibility of what sales was planning to sell and when they expected the orders to come in. The company's customer service manager told us that the MPS with ATP function was the single most important element in their MRP II implementation project for developing a working relationship between the sales and marketing and manufacturing organizations.

In companies where the order promising system used by sales and marketing is linked to the MPS and ATP functions, promised delivery dates are made with a high degree of credibility. These companies have developed the following positions on order promising, which are shared by sales and marketing, manufacturing, and management alike:

1. *A respect for the integrity of a customer promise.* The company adopts an attitude in which sales and marketing, manufacturing, engineering, and management believe that delivery promises are made to be kept.

2. *Well-defined customer service objectives.* The company establishes objectives and monitors the company's performance to those objectives from its customers' perspectives. In measuring its performance, the company asks: How often do we fulfill our promises? How do our promises compare with the delivery date originally requested by the customer?

3. *Accurate records.* For the available-to-promise function to yield reliable promise dates, the company recognizes that the integrity of the data in the MRP system is essential. Bills of material and inventory records must be accurate, and manufacturing must consistently meet the production requirements in the MPS.

4. *Feasible Master Production Schedules.* The company understands that if it promises orders based on a master schedule that is impossible to meet, it is guaranteed to miss the promised delivery dates. Overstated and front-end loaded master schedules torpedo efforts to maintain the integrity of the MPS (see figure 6.5).

5. *Use of promising tools.* When logic is included in the MPS for computing available-to-promise figures and this information is made visible to sales and marketing, reliable delivery promises result.

6. *Procedures for managing abnormal demands.* The company recognizes that large unexpected orders will reduce the availability of product that may have been planned for regular customers. Procedures are developed to process abnormal demands and minimize the poten-

Figure 6.5

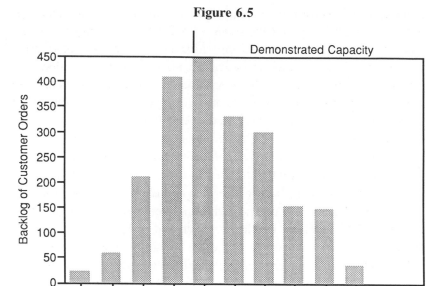

An example of a front-end loaded schedule with late customer orders. Manufacturing cannot ship orders on time, nor will it meet the delivery dates promised on many of the future orders. More orders are scheduled than manufacturing can produce in the near time frames.

tial ill effects to the rest of the company's customers. These procedures will be discussed in more detail later in the chapter.

WHAT DO YOU DO WHEN THE ATP SAYS NO?

Care must be taken to ensure that the ATP function is not misused by the uneducated or the misinformed. The ATP function is a tool to assist sales and marketing in making the best decisions regarding the allocation of product to customers. It is *not* an excuse to ignore the real business opportunities that arise from time to time.

A salesman for a major manufacturer of computer accessories expressed his frustration with what he perceived to be "the computer making decisions for the company.'' After working for months to get a new account, he placed the order with the factory, only to be told that ''the computer'' could not give him the delivery needed to book the order. His experience is indicative of a company that does not understand how to manage the use of the ATP and Master Production Schedule functions to manage demand. And in managing demand, it is sometimes necessary to override the ATP function.

As this example illustrates, the company had an opportunity to take advantage of new business. When the ATP function indicated a longer lead time than the customer required, this did not mean that the order had to be turned down. Rather, this was an indicator that the company needed to manage the demand, which sometimes will require overriding the ATP function. In managing demand, a flexible system needs to be in place so that you can take advantage of new opportunities. When there are insufficient materials and/or capacity available to meet a particular opportunity, the following should be considered:

1. *Trading one customer order for another.* Sometimes, in order to take advantage of unique marketing opportunities, the sales department may wish to schedule a customer order within a time frame that's already booked to capacity. First, the master scheduler should try to adjust the production schedules in the factory to meet the demand. If the master scheduler cannot accommodate the order, however, all is not lost. MRP II systems give sales the information it needs to take advantage of the opportunity by allowing the new order to displace an order already promised. With sales' knowledge of the customers' real needs, existing customer orders may often be renegotiated and rescheduled while minimizing negative impact with other customers. In such cases, the ATP will have told you that it is necessary to swap orders if the other customer promises are to be met (see figure 6.6). When presented with this situation, it is vitally important that sales and marketing work with the master scheduler to consider the impact on other customer orders when making the decision on which orders to swap.

2. *How to fill emergency orders.* It is usually sound policy, and may even be a mandatory business requirement, to interrupt normal priorities to service emergency demand. Filling emergency orders will usually require some juggling of in-house orders to maintain

Figure 6.6

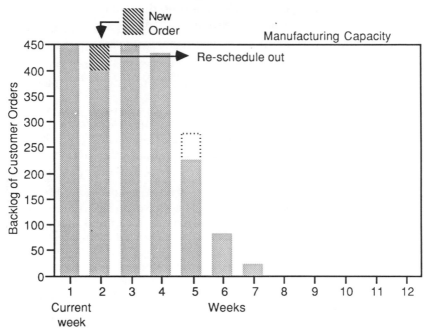

A new order would have to be scheduled in week 5; otherwise, another order or orders would have to be rescheduled.

the integrity of the MPS, and the ATP data will be adjusted accordingly.

3. *What to do when the marketplace demands a specific lead time.* From a marketing point of view, it may be necessary to promise orders by a specific date. When this occurs, it is important to know the impact these orders may have on manufacturing capacity and materials. You must ask: Are you overloading the MPS? What will happen to your on-time delivery to other customers if you accept the order? Can you trade the order with that of another customer, who doesn't require this delivery date? Can you induce the customer to relax his delivery request?

How to Handle Abnormal Demand

Abnormal demand is demand that is unexpected and therefore not forecast. Often, it is not expected to recur. Abnormal demand poses

Figure 6.7
Sample of policies and procedures for
managing abnormal demand

Policy:
  Abnormal demands will be identified, communicated, and managed.

Procedure:
  Abnormal demands will be identified and communicated by the sales, marketing, and customer service departments. This will normally occur at the time of proposal or at order entry. Therefore, all orders will be coded as normal or abnormal demand. Suspect orders will be questioned by the master scheduler.

  Once communicated, abnormal demands will be managed to ensure that the company's customer service, backlog/lead time, inventory, and sales objectives are balanced with the desire to book an unanticipated order. The master scheduler, customer service manager, and demand manager will work together to take advantage of abnormal demand opportunities. They will involve sales, marketing, manufacturing, and other departmental managers as necessary to resolve areas of conflict that may occur. Special Sales and Operations Planning meetings will be called if the abnormal demands would cause the production plan to be exceeded (refer to the Sales and Operations Planning policy) or if conflicts cannot be resolved.

  Demands will be reviewed to determine whether they are normal or abnormal according to the following guidelines: [list your guidelines below]

Note: These guidelines will vary, depending on the specific customer and company situation. In fact, the specific guidelines that you establish are less important than the fact that you are creating guidelines at all. Change the guidelines as experience dictates. Following are some sample guidelines that are commonly employed:

Examples:
1. Any demand that requires equal or greater than n percent of the forecast in any one time period will be reviewed.

2. All proposals in excess of $n.nn will be reviewed.

3. Significant orders for "low volume" products will be reviewed.

4. All new customers with orders in excess of $n.nn will be followed up by sales personnel.

  All orders classified as *abnormal* will be summed up and analyzed every six months. A report will be issued at the regular Sales and Operations Planning meeting. This activity will help everyone better understand the predictability of the marketplace. Further, it will point out areas where additional attention is needed to improve the sales plan.

both an opportunity and a challenge. Because it is usually unanticipated, it is not included in the company's sales plans or manufacturing plans. Therein lies the opportunity. The challenge is to fulfill the abnormal demand without adversely affecting your company's performance with other customers; agreeing to accept the abnormal demand can alter availability, lead times, inventory levels, and capacity and material plans.

Managing abnormal demand is one of the major responsibilities of the sales and marketing organizations (see figure 6.8). By definition, every abnormal demand is an opportunity, since it is business you have not counted upon to make this year's plan. It is the job of sales and marketing to identify abnormal demand and communicate the prospects to management, manufacturing, and, particularly, to the master scheduler. Sales and marketing can communicate the opportunity of abnormal demands in advance by specifically forecasting a segment of "unexpected" demand, which gives manufacturing the opportunity to plan for capacity and raw materials even though it is not possible to specifically forecast what the order contains or when it will be required.

When presented with the opportunity of abnormal demand, sales and marketing cannot simply "throw the order over the wall" to manufacturing and expect them to service the order without adversely affecting other customers in the plan. By working with manufacturing to manage the backlog of orders, schedule ship dates, and prioritize orders, you can take advantage of unexpected business opportunities while minimizing the negative effect on other orders.

IDENTIFYING ABNORMAL DEMAND

The sales force and customer service department are usually the first to become aware of abnormal demands at the time of request for quotation or when the order is placed. Consequently, they are in the best position to notify manufacturing and marketing personnel, and especially the people responsible for demand management, of the abnormal demand.

To ensure that abnormal demand and its impact on other customer

Figure 6.8

Abnormal demands are both an opportunity and a challenge to a manufacturing company. The opportunity is incremental business. The challenge is to *manage* the company's customer service to other customers.

orders is not overlooked in the planning system, the following criteria may be used by sales and marketing personnel to identify, and then communicate, the abnormal demand:

1. The customer order is large compared with the amount of available products either from inventory or from the Master Production Schedule.

2. The order is large when compared with the detailed product forecast.

3. The order is received from a new customer, either as the result

of a long-term, diligent sales effort, or a competitor's inability to supply the product, or both.

4. The order is from a customer whose business is not forecasted in the current sales plan. Unplanned business can result from business that was not previously visible, such as an order placed by the government on a classified project.

5. The volume of business from a regular customer significantly exceeds the sales plan for that customer. Additional business from an established customer may be the result of abnormal demand that is not likely to recur or an unusual requirement that your customer did not even anticipate.

MANAGING ABNORMAL DEMAND

A manufacturer of safety valves received an unanticipated request to supply product to a fertilizer processing plant that was being constructed in India. Since the company had not known the plant was being constructed, the order was not in its sales or production plans. Nevertheless, the order could represent a significant increase in earnings in the third quarter.

The company decided to accept the order, but did not use demand management techniques to analyze the order's impact on fulfilling other promised orders. Consequently, the master scheduler first became aware of the order when capacity and materials were overpromised. Manufacturing managers were told that overtime was going to be necessary; however, the manufacturing organization was already working overtime. Also, purchasing was unable to arrange for components used in the valves to be received in time to meet the customer's promised delivery date. As a result, the unexpected order and many of the company's previously promised orders were delivered late, so that the new customer and some established customers did not receive the service expected—the service that had been promised. Further, the late shipments caused a shortfall in projected third quarter earnings.

The master scheduler lamented to the manufacturing manager, "If only the salesman had told us as soon as he learned about the prospect for the order, we could have started planning, renegotiated some delivery dates with vendors, arranged for additional capacity, and renegotiated some existing customer delivery dates.''

The salesman was heard telling his sales manager, ''Why can't manufacturing respond more quickly? Now I have to explain to four customers why their orders were late. I hope we don't lose any customers because of this.''

At the next management meeting, when the general manager asked why customer service was so poor, the sales manager and manufacturing manager got into a heated argument.

Fortunately, however, there's a happy ending to the story, and the company's sales manager and manufacturing manager now cite the India fertilizer plant order as a turning point for the company. It proved to be the impetus for the establishment of using demand management techniques and a formal system for identifying and communicating abnormal demand. Today, when abnormal demand is identified by either sales or customer service personnel, it is used to:

1. Guide order promising discussions.
2. Assist in the forecasting/demand planning process.
3. Assist in the Sales and Operations Planning process.
4. Provide information to sales and marketing for potential new business opportunities.

The master scheduler is no longer the first person to begin analyzing the impact of unanticipated orders on the company's materials and capacity. The abnormal demand is analyzed at the detail level and the management level, as appropriate, before the order is accepted.

Most companies will very naturally accept the order, just as the valve manufacturer did. When a company manages abnormal demand by using the Master Production Schedule with its available-to-promise function, it can make a better-informed decision about what terms are acceptable for the order. Managing abnormal demand enables you to negotiate from a position of knowledge prior to committing delivery dates to customers. In addition to giving manufacturing the chance to resolve supply problems, it also gives sales and marketing the opportunity to review existing and anticipated customer orders to minimize the impact of the unexpected order on customer service performance.

If the abnormal demand is of sufficient size, it may be necessary to add capacity to the manufacturing or engineering organization, or hire a subcontractor to perform some of the work. When abnormal demand adds significantly to the overall manufacturing plan, then manufacturing will need to offer alternatives to management during the Sales and Operations Planning process for meeting the demand. In that case, sales and marketing will have to answer two key questions during the process of reviewing alternatives:

1. Is this unanticipated demand really a one-time event, or can we expect to receive this level of demand in the future?
2. If we change priorities to satisfy this demand, which customer or product priorities should we change?

The answers to these questions guide the company in making the best use of its resources in satisfying all customer demand, whether abnormal or planned. The abnormal demand information is also useful in increasing the accuracy of forecasts when using sales history to project the future, especially when an automated forecasting software package is being used. Demand that is determined to be nonrecurring can be excluded from the forecast history so that one-time demands do not skew the forecast of anticipated demand (see figure 6.9).

When a formal system is used to identify, communicate, and manage abnormal demand, it often can be used to enable sales and marketing to identify new business opportunities. The orders from a new customer or a market for a new application may become a major source of incremental business for sales and marketing to pursue. If the abnormal demand is the result of a competitor's problems, there might be a great opportunity for increasing market share. In either case, timely identification and communication of abnormal demand are needed to take advantage of these situations.

FORECAST CONSUMPTION

The issue of consuming the forecast must be addressed when developing MPS policies. An inevitable reality is that timing of actual cus-

Figure 6.9

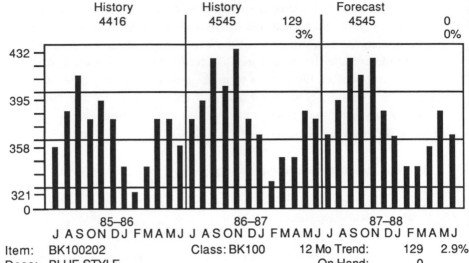

	History 4416		History 4545	129 3%		Forecast 4545	0 0%

Item: BK100202   Class: BK100   12 Mo Trend: 129   2.9%
Desc: BLUE STYLE   On Hand: 0
Cost: · 145.000   Price: 378.000   Safety Stock: 0
Form: 7   07/01   Error: 3.5 −3.1   Lead Time: 0   Days

(G) raph Annually / (R) oll Back / i History Screen . .

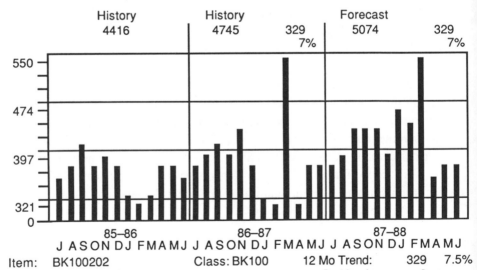

Item: BK100202   Class: BK100   12 Mo Trend: 329   7.5%
Desc: BLUE STYLE   On Hand: 0
Cost: 145.000   Price: 378.000   Safety Stock: 0
Form: 20   07/01   Error: 3.9 −1.0   Lead Time: 0   Days

(G) raph Annually / (R) oll Back / i History Screen . .

The data displayed show the effect of a large abnormal demand on the Focus Forecast. The upper graph shows the forecast without the abnormal demand. The bottom graph shows the forecast with the abnormal demand. Note that both the quantity and timing of forecasted demand have been affected. (Courtesy of Decision Technologies, Inc., Clayton, Mo.)

tomer orders will not be identical to the forecast. Consequently, the question must be answered: How will timing variances be handled when the computer system updates its records for the passage of time?

Many computer systems update their MRP information weekly, though the available-to-promise information is usually updated more frequently, typically daily. Depending on how timing variances are handled, a forecast communicated via the Master Production Schedule may change with every computer update. It is important that before a forecast is changed, the reasons for making the changes are understood. This analysis cannot be performed by the computer system—it requires human judgment.

Some computer systems automatically change the forecast when timing variances occur. We strongly advise against permitting the computer system to change the forecast without first having marketing decide whether that change is desirable or necessary.

For example, a sales plan for selling four hundred units of Product A per month has been established and input into the computer system. Once a week, the computer system is updated for the passage of time (one week). During the past week, although one hundred units were originally forecast, twenty units have not been sold (see figure 6.10). That is, twenty units remain in the forecast, so actual demand was twenty units less than forecasted. Most software systems will simply drop the twenty unsold units as the records are updated for the passage of time. The unsold twenty units disappear from all calculations, thus reducing the monthly forecast from 400 to 380. Dropping the unsold units from the forecast may make sense, if you are convinced that the twenty units will not sell and the monthly sales plan is to be reduced. If the forecast *quantity* was correct, but only the *timing* was incorrect, you will want to keep the twenty units in the forecast.

In the situation described above, the actual demand falls behind the forecast in time. It is just as likely that the actual demand could lead the forecast. Your software logic will need to be able to handle both situations.

The forecast consumption issue has been a source of grief for many companies, which unwittingly change their forecasts every week on all their master scheduled items. When the computer is updated and automatically makes changes to the forecast for time variances, the mas-

Figure 6.10

Product A

|←———— 400 ————→| = 4 week anticipated demand

	1	2	3	4	5	6	7	8
Forecast	20	30	80	90	100	100	100	
Actual Demand	80	70	20	10	0	0	0	
Total	100	100	100	100	100	100	100	

↑ 20 Remain to be sold

The original forecast of 400 will be reduced by 20 if the computer drops the remaining 20 when it updates its records. Be sure your software logic accounts for the *timing* of demand.

ter scheduler can receive an overabundance of messages that require evaluation and decisions on action to be taken. When the number of messages is large enough, we refer to the Master Production Schedule as being "nervous." Often, there are too many messages for the master scheduler to adequately evaluate, which causes frustration and often results in poor performance.

We believe that people, rather than the computer system, should be accountable for the forecast. People should make the decision about when the forecast changes, rather than simply allowing the computer system to make the changes automatically.

MASTER SCHEDULER: FRIEND OR FOE?

Before we move on to discuss sales' and marketing's requirements for the order entry function, we'd like to make one final note about master schedulers. Are they the friend or foe of sales and marketing?

Too often we believe they are viewed as the foe, and made the scapegoat—particularly when delivery dates are missed. This usually occurs when sales and marketing personnel hold a narrow view of the master scheduler and Master Production Schedule's function. When this view prevails, internal dissension arises and wastes valuable time and energy needed to combat the real enemy—the competition.

When sales and marketing understand the master scheduler's role and responsibility, this understanding can be the foundation for cooperation and teamwork. The master scheduler is responsible for:

1. Participating in developing manufacturing's input to Sales and Operations Planning.
2. Maintaining an attainable MPS by monitoring the consistency of the production plan, maintaining planning bills, protecting the MPS data integrity, executing policies for time fences, safety stocks, subcontracting, and lot sizing.
3. Managing the Master Production Schedule and forecast consumption.
4. Identifying, negotiating, and resolving conflicts on material and capacity availability and order promising integrity.
5. Working with sales and marketing to satisfy customer demand.

Because the master scheduler is the person who determines what the company will build and what will be available to sell, he or she is the key person for sales and marketing—particularly the demand manager—to work with to determine how demand will be managed at the detail level. For example, about a year after Bently Nevada became a Class A MRP II manufacturer, our international sales manager notified us of a large order that was available. Although the sales organization had pursued the order for a long time, we had not anticipated receiving it within this time frame. We also had been pessimistic about the customer selecting Bently Nevada to supply the order, as our price was significantly higher than our competitors'. But the customer offered the order to us, at our price, *if we could meet their delivery date.*

The requested delivery was less than our normal delivery lead times. But our customer service manager and master scheduler worked together to determine how we would be able to accept the order at the customer's requested delivery date while minimizing the impact on other customer orders. The result of sales and marketing and manufacturing's working together on the order was increased business, continued excellent customer service to established customers, and on-time delivery to the new customer and other customers as well.

ORDER ENTRY

We discussed earlier in this chapter the importance of linking the system sales uses to enter orders to the system manufacturing uses to schedule orders, via the Master Production Schedule. When these systems are linked, MRP II becomes more of a company system, rather than just a manufacturing system.

Companies sometimes tend to look at order entry as a stand-alone function rather than as a fundamental part of their company's operating system. This narrow viewpoint can present obstacles to achieving the company's customer service objectives. A broader viewpoint, which includes ATP as previously discussed, is needed to meet customer-service objectives.

We regularly see companies where the forecasters do not have sufficient data to use as a basis for forecasting. Often, the reason for insufficient data is that this data is not captured through the order entry system and is not maintained in the customer master file. For example, customer request date is a key piece of information to capture at order entry if a company is to understand and forecast *demand* versus bookings or shipments. When an order entry system is not designed to capture and save this type of key marketing data, the forecaster will be hampered by the historical data base in making forecasting decisions.

Another problem some companies face is that as their MRP II efforts become effective, manufacturing lead times may be reduced to the point where order entry time becomes a significant part of the customer delivery lead time. We were confronted with this situation at Bently Nevada after achieving Class A MRP II status, and it soon became obvious that we were missing an opportunity to improve customer service performance because of inefficiencies and inaccuracies in our order entry system.

Sales and marketing, manufacturing, and management agreed that there had to be a better way of entering orders. We established a Customer Order Service project under the direction of Jim Prevatte, a member of the MRP II project team, and the order entry system was upgraded to link directly to the company's MRP II system. By thinking of the order entry system as a natural extension or part of the company's MRP II system, we adopted a broader approach to the order entry function, which we viewed as having three primary purposes:

1. Communicating actual customer orders to manufacturing.
2. Communicating delivery information to customers.
3. Communicating customer information to sales and marketing for improving demand planning.

After identifying the objectives of the new order entry system, we developed the following key criteria for the system:

1. The order entry's promising function will be linked to the Master Production Schedule's available-to-promise function and inventory data. By tying these systems together, sales and marketing can know what is truly available-to-promise and can make more accurate delivery promises to customers.

2. Data required for demand planning will be entered into the order entry system. In addition to the usual marketing and customer data, these data will include the customer request date to capture real customer demand, unconstrained by the company's delivery lead times. Other data to be included are promised delivery date, actual shipped date, abnormal demand, and demand stream data.

3. The system will be designed to eliminate the amount of time required to enter orders, minimize order entry errors, and communicate demand information to manufacturing and engineering.

4. The system will be designed to improve the company's performance in the eyes of the customer. Specifically, it will enable customer questions to be answered quickly regarding order status, delivery, and availability. It also will provide on-line available-to-promise information to the company's major regional sales offices as well as to customer service representatives at corporate headquarters.

5. The system will interface with the company's financial system for more efficient and accurate invoicing and financial planning.

Companies often find themselves in a position similar to ours at Bently Nevada, where the order entry system was not considered until after the rest of the MRP II system was in place. But once the manufacturing and financial portions of the MRP II system are in place, order entry begins to receive attention. Bill Sandras, of Productivity Centers International and an Oliver Wight Education Associate, tells us that his clients who are implementing JIT consistently find that ''order entry inevitably becomes one of the next big rocks.'' His experience, like ours, shows that most order entry processes take considerable time, have many errors that result in change orders, and often operate on separate data bases.

Sales and marketing must not only address these issues if the company is to achieve long-term competitiveness in its marketplace, but they also must lead the process to ensure that the order entry system incorporates the features, functions, and information required by sales and marketing to communicate effectively with manufacturing, improve efficiency, and gather the data needed to make more reliable forecasts.

During the planning and development of a new order entry system, it is advantageous to review your marketing/manufacturing strategy. The company should reconsider:

1. What do customers expect?
2. What will be required to compete?
3. How can the company gain an edge?
4. Within what time period should the company make accurate delivery promises? One day? One minute? One week?
5. How does the company wish to appear in the eyes of the customer?
6. Should order status be immediately available?
7. How many people at what locations need to make delivery promises to customers or check the status of customer orders?
8. How does the company wish to forecast, plan, and schedule its business?

During the development of an order entry system, sales and marketing should lead the process of determining the logic, language, and any error checking employed by the system. Order entry software will most often require some modification to meet your specific requirements.

For order entry systems to be truly effective, they must speak the language of their users. Consequently, it is not unusual to find that order entry systems include "translators." These translators enable the order entry system to speak the users' language by recognizing customers' ordering numbers, the company's selling, or catalog, numbers, and manufacturing planning and scheduling numbers.

In addition to translators, a well-designed order entry system includes logic for error checking and error prevention to minimize mistakes and omissions during the order entry process. An example of this would be order entry systems that don't allow for the input of incompatible product options.

CHECKLIST

1. Does your company have a valid Master Production Schedule?
2. Has a Master Production Scheduling Policy been established that covers:
   a. How customer orders will be promised?
   b. What time fences will be used?
   c. Under what authority will changes in customer priorities be made?
   d. What is specifically included in the MPS?
   e. Who is responsible for providing a detailed forecast to the master scheduler?
   f. How performance to the master schedule will be measured?

3. Does the MPS include an available-to-promise function?
4. Is the order promising system used by sales and marketing linked to the MPS and ATP functions?
5. Is demand managed when the ATP function shows insufficient product in the MPS to take advantage of business opportunities?
6. Do sales and marketing actively manage abnormal demand?
7. Has the issue of consuming the forecast been addressed?
8. Is the master scheduler viewed as a key link, rather than an adversary, in determining how demand will be managed at the detail level?
9. Is the order entry system linked to the operating system?

Chapter 7

Demand Analysis: Reducing Uncertainty of Demand

> *We don't have any trouble forecasting. Our forecasts are always 100 percent accurate. The trouble is, our customers don't read our forecasts.*
> **—CEO's lament**

We have discussed how to predict, communicate, influence, and manage demand. This is done for one underlying purpose: to reduce the uncertainty of demand.

Why is reducing the uncertainty of demand important, if not paramount, to gaining the marketing edge? The answer is simple: the more certain you are of demand, the better your company can perform. When demand is uncertain, the manufacturing, engineering, and support organizations in a company are handicapped in their efforts to provide a quality product at a low cost, and deliver it to the customer on time. In some cases these organizations simply don't have enough time to truly concentrate on improving quality, cost, and delivery. The more uncertain the demand, the more their time and energy is devoted to coping with unexpected but inevitable changes.

To demonstrate how your company can gain a marketing edge through demand management, this book has addressed the following major issues:

- *Marketing/manufacturing strategy* for meeting customer expected lead times, given manufacturing lead times.

133

- *Sales and Operations Planning* for operating the company as a team, based on one game plan and one set of numbers.
- *Forecasting* of anticipated demand for use as input to the planning process.
- *Sales planning* to gain commitment to sell the plan.
- *Master Production Scheduling* for turning plans into reality.

When companies address the issues outlined above, they establish a framework for success. But to remain truly competitive, this framework alone is not enough. There must be a continual effort to reduce the uncertainty of demand. This chapter will present techniques for achieving continual improvement in reducing the uncertainty of demand. These techniques include demand stream analysis, Distribution Resource Planning (DRP), Total Quality Control (TQC), methods for coping with the uncertainty of demand, and measurements and feedback. When these techniques are applied, you can improve your company's understanding of the marketplace, better communicate demand information and plans, and improve the execution of sales plans.

HOW TO IMPROVE PREDICTIONS OF DEMAND

In chapter 4, we discussed in detail the forecasting process. You can improve your ability to forecast anticipated demand and reduce the uncertainty of demand by concentrating on four key issues:

1. *Proper attention.* This involves using skilled people at the proper level in the company to achieve success.
2. *Frequency of review and update.* This requires continuous review and update by the demand planner, who reviews, presents, and updates the forecast at least once a month.
3. *Different views.* Reconciling different views of the market during the demand planning process by asking questions about the factors and assumptions behind the numbers.
4. *Measurements.* It has been said that whatever you measure will improve. This concept certainly holds true for improving forecasts and sales plan performance.

DEMAND STREAM ANALYSIS FOR IMPROVED PREDICTIONS

A significant opportunity exists in many companies for reducing the uncertainty of demand through a more detailed analysis of the source of demand. Often in the forecasting process, demand for product is treated as though it came from one homogeneous demand stream. In reality, however, most demands can be separated into independent demand streams. By separating demands into streams, you gain a better understanding of the business and an improved ability to forecast, plan, and manage by individual demand stream.

For example, a plastics manufacturer on the West Coast was plagued by inaccurate forecasts. The company's general manager finally requested that the forecasting errors be analyzed. Were the inaccuracies the result of the logic employed by the forecasting software? Were the data input into the software invalid? Should the company buy new software, hire a new forecaster?

Through an analysis of why its forecasts were unreliable, the company determined that the software functioned properly, the demand data input into the forecasting program were correct (they considered the timing difference between shipments, bookings, and demand), and the forecaster was aggressively working to improve the forecast. The root cause of the forecasting inaccuracies was that the company did not understand the various demand streams that made up its aggregate demand. Erratic demand was traced to three product lines and to two large volume customers. These customers routinely increased or decreased their orders with the company on short notice. Also, one of the market segments the company served was experiencing a downturn in business. The company had not analyzed markets by segment in developing sales plans and forecasts. Finally, a new product was more popular than anticipated, and customers were ordering fewer of the older version of the product and more of the new one. All of these issues were contributing to inaccurate forecasts.

To avoid these problems in the future, the company began using a more structured approach for analyzing demand. The following steps were taken:

Figure 7.1

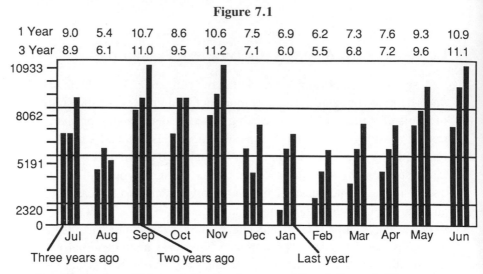

| 1 Year | 9.0 | 5.4 | 10.7 | 8.6 | 10.6 | 7.5 | 6.9 | 6.2 | 7.3 | 7.6 | 9.3 | 10.9 |
| 3 Year | 8.9 | 6.1 | 11.0 | 9.5 | 11.2 | 7.1 | 6.0 | 5.5 | 6.8 | 7.2 | 9.6 | 11.1 |

Graphic display of history, showing the seasonality of demand. Three years of history are displayed on an annual format showing demand by month. An index of demand per month is shown at the top for the last year and the past three years.

1. *Analysis of aggregate demand history.* The history (in aggregate) was viewed in graphic format to determine overall trends and seasonality of demand (see figure 7.1).

2. *Segmentation of demand history into demand streams.* The purpose of this analysis was to determine the source of demand by individual market, territory, customer, and product.

3. *Analysis of segmented demand streams over the same time period.* This analysis enabled the company to identify seasonality and trends by individual demand stream.

Most companies perform market segmentation when developing annual marketing and sales plans. What many fail to develop, however, is a detailed time-phased product forecast by segment, which plays a major role in reducing the uncertainty of demand. It is common for some segments to be either increasing or decreasing in demand when compared with the overall business plan. An analysis of demand by segment helps ensure that the time-phased sum of all segments equals the time-phased total of the sales plan in the Sales and Operations Plan.

DEMAND STREAM ANALYSIS FOR INFLUENCING DEMAND

Understanding the company's different demand streams also affords you the opportunity to *manage* each stream appropriately. You may have a market segment that accepts a longer lead time and, in fact, allows you to operate on a make-to-order basis for some products. You also may have another demand stream that must be serviced out of finished goods inventory. By separating these different demand streams, you can set different delivery lead time objectives and inventory level objectives for each one. In essence, you can manage each demand stream to achieve its independent customer service objectives.

We recently talked with a manufacturer who does a significant volume of business outside the United States and is greatly affected by the changing value of the U.S. dollar. To better manage the situation, the company separates international and domestic demand and handles them as separate product families in the Sales and Operations Planning process, even though the product is the same when viewed from manufacturing's point of view. By separating the demand streams, the company greatly improved both the visibility of demand and its ability to anticipate demand. As the value of the dollar changed, the forecast for international demands could be updated easily. Additionally, since the product was visibly independent from the other product families, performance could be measured against the plan, and resources could be specifically allocated to international demand versus domestic demand.

We're familiar with another manufacturer that markets its products directly to users and through original equipment manufacturers (OEMs). For demand planning purposes, this company looks at the business as separate parts, according to marketing channel, because there is a significant difference in price, depending upon which channel the product is sold through.

DISTRIBUTION RESOURCE PLANNING

Companies with branch warehouses or large distributors can gain better visibility of demand through the use of Distribution Resource

Planning (DRP). DRP has proved to be an excellent tool for managing distribution inventories and all their associated resources. It is particularly valuable for companies that ship many products to many warehouses and distributors and is useful for any company with distributed inventories.

DRP provides a communication link between warehouses and the factory, and it is used by the demand planner, the distribution organization, and the master scheduler. It ensures that distribution demand is included in the demand planning process and provides forward visibility of time-phased demand for planning purposes. Any company with distributed inventories is strongly encouraged to read *DRP: Distribution Management's Most Powerful Tool*, by André Martin, a DRP pioneer and Oliver Wight Education Associate, who has assisted businesses throughout the country in the implementation of DRP.

A hardware supplier in the Midwest and a computer manufacturer on the West Coast are two excellent examples of companies achieving success with DRP. The hardware supply company uses DRP to manage its demand and control its purchases from vendors. The company's inventory control manager remarked, "DRP lets us plan for the future and thereby control the inbound flow of material into our warehouses. Before DRP, we launched orders and expedited problems. Now, we control those orders."

The computer manufacturer uses DRP to measure activities at its distribution centers. The company knows, by the minute, how many customer orders are coming in, how many orders are being picked and packed, and how many orders are being shipped. This information allows the company to anticipate, rather than react to, change.

André Martin has been working with CXA Ltd. of Brownsburg, Quebec, Canada, on implementing their DRP system with CXA's customers. CXA, a manufacturer of explosive devices, is also actively working toward becoming a Class A MRP II user. CXA markets exclusively through its distributors and has twelve major distributors on line with its DRP communications system. CXA plans to have all key distributors on line within nine to twelve months of this writing, according to Morris Bannerman, director of marketing.

CXA's DRP system not only communicates time-phased anticipated demand information, but it also provides a time-phased model of inventory and a suggested order profile. This dynamic model projects and anticipates future shortages and recommends action in the form of suggested order quantities in a time-phased manner.

When such a model is used, it enables sales and marketing to have their customers forecast their own business for the company. This is valuable in building and maintaining positive relationships with customers. Could your company employ this technique with its customers? Think about the following comment from Theodore Levitt of the Harvard Business School:

> A company's most precious asset is its relationship with its customers. The seller's ability to forecast the buyer's intentions rests on the quality of the overall relationship. In a good relationship, the buyer shares plans and expectations with the vendor, or at least makes available relevant information. With that information the vendor can better serve the buyer. Surprises and bad forecasts are symptoms of bad relationships. In such instances, even the buyer loses.

How to Continuously Reduce the Uncertainty of Demand

We mentioned Total Quality Control (TQC) in chapter 1. In this chapter, we will provide a brief overview of some of the principles of TQC and TQC techniques that can be used to help reduce the uncertainty of demand.

TQC is a systematic approach to solving problems. Just-in-Time (JIT) is used to identify problems; TQC is used to isolate the root cause of problems so that solutions can be developed. Statistical Process Control is an effective and popular means of improving quality through the control of a process. Many nonstatistical techniques are also available to assist in this systematic approach to solving problems.

Using the Pareto Chart

One of the most useful TQC tools for analyzing and solving problems is Pareto's law. Also known as the "80/20 rule," this analysis is

Figure 7.2

Pareto Analysis

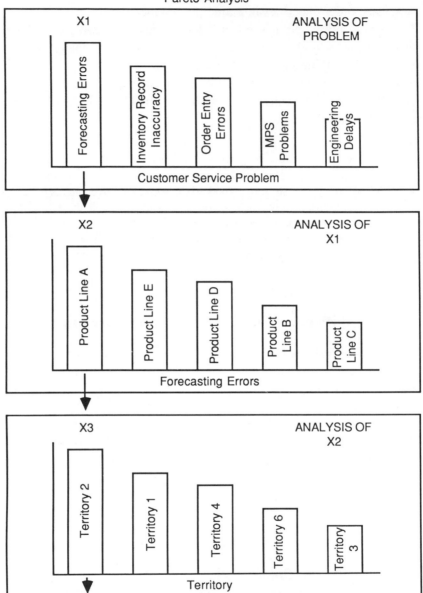

Using Pareto's law to analyze problems.

Figure 7.2 (continued)

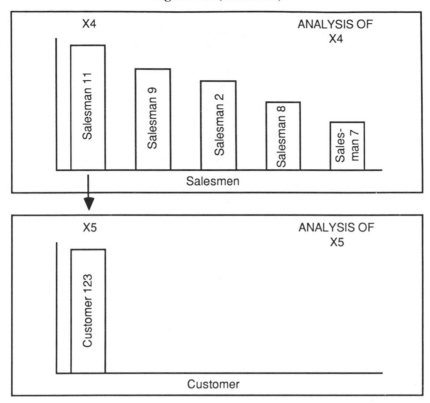

Using Pareto's law to analyze problems.

based upon the rule developed by Vilfredo Pareto, an Italian economist of the late 1800s, who stated, ''Where there are a large number of contributors to a result, the majority of the result is due to a minority of contributors.''

Pareto's law can be useful for isolating the root cause of problems. First, the potential causes of a problem are identified and the frequency of their occurrence is measured. The causes that contribute most to the problem are further analyzed by applying the same Pareto approach, and this is continued as many times as is needed until the root cause of the problem is determined. Generally, the information identified through the first two levels of Pareto analysis represent *symptoms* of the prob-

Figure 7.3

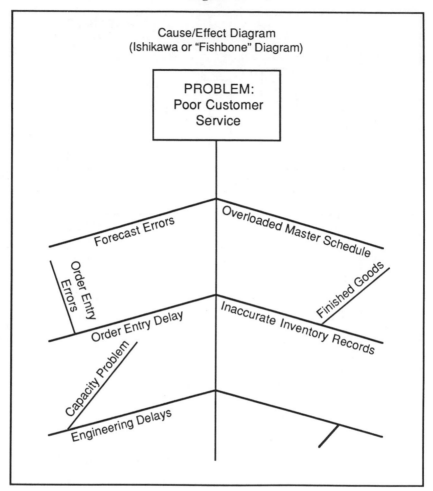

An Ishikawa, or ''fishbone,'' diagram. The ''ribs'' list possible causes of the problem.

lem. The Pareto analysis is commonly used through four or five levels to identify the root cause of the problem (see figure 7.2).

The following example will show how a Pareto analysis can be used to reduce the uncertainty of demand. Let's say your company's sales organization has determined there is a customer service problem. At the first level of Pareto analysis, you determine the possible causes of the problem by using another TQC tool, the Ishikawa, or "fishbone," diagram (see figure 7.3). Next, you begin to make measurements to gather *facts* about each possible cause identified in the fishbone analysis. As you monitor, measure, and log the causes of the customer service problem, you determine that forecast errors are the largest single contributor to the problem.

To determine the cause of these forecast errors, you follow the same procedure of using the fishbone diagram and measurements. This analysis reveals that the single largest forecast error occurs in one product line. To analyze the cause of forecasting errors in this product line, you again use the fishbone analysis and measurements. At this level of analysis, you determine that error occurs mostly in one sales territory. Further analysis isolates the problem to one salesperson, and, then to one large-volume customer who frequently orders at the last moment with little advance warning (see figure 7.4). Your suborganization probes deeper, and you learn this customer is willing to participate in a customer linking program in which it shares its planned purchases with you, a measure that will help reduce the problem. As you can see from this example, simple, easy-to-implement TQC tools are available to identify and correct the root cause of demand management problems.

ANALYZING THE SPARE PARTS DEMAND STREAM

When analyzing demand streams, spare parts, custom engineered products, and new products are sometimes overlooked or planned outside the formal planning system. Yet, in some companies, they comprise a significant percentage of the business. For this reason, a process for handling these demand streams needs to be developed. Demand for spare parts can be difficult to plan at the Sales and Operations Planning level because there are typically too many numbers to forecast across numerous product families and too little time for management to review. To further complicate the issue, the same spare parts are often used in numerous products.

Nevertheless, an attempt must be made to manage the demand for

Figure 7.4

```
┌─────────────────────────────────────────┐
│                                         │
│           Measurements of               │
│           Problem/Cause                 │
│           Occurences                    │
│                                         │
│   Forecast Error              ‖‖‖ ‖‖‖ |  │
│   Order Entry Error           |||       │
│   Master Production Schedule            │
│      Overload                 ||        │
│   Inventory Record Error      ||||      │
│   Engineering Delays          ‖‖‖       │
│                                         │
└─────────────────────────────────────────┘
```

Checklist providing input for Pareto analysis of a customer service problem.

spare parts. To this end, some firms have had success in creating separate product families at the Sales and Operations Planning level to handle this demand. Other companies simply review their historical data based on shipments or past demand, and adjust percentages on planning bills accordingly. Still other companies rely more heavily on forecasting software, sales history, and installed product base to forecast spare parts at the individual item level.

CUSTOM-ENGINEERED PRODUCTS

Another class of products that is frequently overlooked in demand planning is custom-engineered products. We are not referring here to companies whose primary business is engineered products, like aerospace and defense companies. We are referring to companies in which a portion of the business may be custom-engineered for strategic or tactical reasons. Companies may offer custom-engineered products because they don't want to give up any business to their competitors. In some companies, a portion of their business is custom products. Unfortunately, these companies often do not pay the same amount of attention to planning and scheduling the custom business as they do to their mainline business. When they don't plan and schedule their custom business, they can cause problems not only in the custom area but in the mainline business if the custom business utilizes the same manufacturing resources.

Engineered products can be planned, however, whether they're your primary business or not. When scheduling engineered products, capacity planning of the engineering resource should be considered, because you're not only planning and scheduling materials and manufacturing capacities, but your planning the engineering staff's time as well.

In some companies, the volume of engineering business is small compared with the volume of business from its standard product lines. For this reason, capacity planning of engineering resources is often overlooked. When customer service problems arise, however, analysis of the situation frequently shows that the source of the customer service problem is an overloaded engineering department. Analyzing the demand on engineering resources and including engineering resources in the Sales and Operations Planning and Master Production Scheduling processes enable you to take one more step toward reducing the uncertainty of demand, as seen by the supply side of the business.

Other techniques that can assist you in establishing a demand plan for engineered products are rough cut capacity planning and the development of planning bills of material. Resource profiles of the engineered product can be developed from historical data for use in rough cut capacity planning. Planning bills of material can be developed for long lead time materials and other steps in the production cycle, such as engineering and customer approval.

NEW PRODUCTS

Forecasting and scheduling new products are especially difficult because the demand is dependent on customers' acceptance of the new product, which may not yet be known. Also, the product itself often changes throughout the engineering development process, so the necessary manufacturing processes, materials, and capacities will not be known precisely. Further adding to the difficulty of performing demand planning for new products is the fact that collateral tasks, such as the development of product literature, need to be scheduled along with product engineering. More schedules mean more uncertainties and increased potential for problems in communicating the demand throughout the company and coordinating the execution of the company's demand strategy for the new product.

Given the difficulties in planning new product introductions, how should you assess new product demand? First of all, new product development must be included in the formal resource planning system early in the project. Frequent review of all schedules is required to coordinate the multiple schedules from various organizations and to adjust them if necessary. Once the product has been introduced, more frequent forecast updates will be required as customer acceptance becomes evident. In general, constant monitoring, management, and attention to detail are needed to reduce the uncertainty of demand for new products as well as to phase out production of products made obsolete by the introduction of the new products.

As we discussed with engineered products, resource profiles and planning bills of material can assist in the planning process for new products. Resource profiles can be developed for rough cut capacity planning. Planning bills may be used to plan for materials with long lead times and may even be used to schedule design engineering, product testing, field sales and service training, and sales promotions.

COPING WITH THE UNCERTAINTY OF DEMAND

After all reasonable efforts have been made to develop and improve demand plans and forecasts, there will still be inaccuracies in the timing or quantity of demand. What do you do when confronted with these inaccuracies, despite your efforts to reduce the uncertainty of demand?

The objective of your efforts is to develop demand plans and forecasts that are reliable enough to operate the business effectively and provide the level of service your customers expect. With this objective in mind, consider the following elements as you plan to cope with the uncertainty of demand:

1. *Lead times.* Perhaps the single most effective way to cope with uncertainty of demand is to reduce, or collapse, all the lead times in

the company. If the company can quickly respond to changes in demand, then forecasts of anticipated demand can be less accurate, and the company can still maintain the same level of customer service. Tremendous benefits come from reducing the lead times needed to produce a product. If your company is not yet actively implementing JIT, with its resulting reduction in lead times, you owe it to your customers to spearhead the effort.

2. *Customer linking.* We addressed customer linking earlier in the discussions on sales planning. It is clear to us that anything you can do to turn your customers' plans into your company's plans is not only desirable but may be necessary if you are to compete in the future. Active pursuit of customer linking with key customers will undoubtedly help reduce the uncertainties of demand.

3. *Safety stock.* Although inventory in itself is wasteful, it is sometimes necessary in order to maintain your customer service objectives. If your demand is unpredictable, and the time required to respond to changes in demand is longer than customer requested lead times, inventory can be used to service the customer. When inventory is being used to service the customer, sales and marketing should be responsible for recommending inventory levels.

One note of caution: using inventory to cover for uncertainty of demand can be expensive and does not always ensure adequate customer service. History has proven that even with high inventory levels, demand often doesn't match the inventory. Sooner or later, the inventory will become old or obsolete due to changes in the product or market. Consequently, inventory must be kept at levels that are as low as practical.

The costs associated with carrying inventory add significantly to the cost of the product and must be reflected in the product's price. It is not uncommon to find companies that estimate the cost of carrying inventory to be between 20 and 30 percent of the inventory value. But if it is necessary to have on hand, inventory can help you cope with the uncertainty of demand.

4. *Safety capacity.* For some companies, capacity rather than materials, is the primary constraint in meeting demand. These companies use safety capacity as a means of coping with the uncertainty of demand. By allowing some flexibility in their Master Production Sched-

ule, they leave some capacity available to ensure that the company provides adequate customer service. As with safety stock, however, safety capacity is expensive and presumes that you have extra labor or machinery for various periods of time.

5. *Sell around the problem.* If customers are not asking for what you have in stock or in the Master Production Schedule, you may have to sell what you do have in stock or are scheduled to produce. Most salespeople are prepared to sell what's in stock or in the schedule— if they know what that is. As we discussed in the section of chapter 6 on available-to-promise, the key is to have a communication system that tells the salespeople what is available to sell.

6. *Backlog.* If the timing of your demand is unpredictable, an effective means of coping with the uncertainty is to carefully manage your company's backlog of orders. Using the available-to-promise function, we recommend that sales and marketing not promise the best possible ship dates when working with customer orders, so as not to lose flexibility in responding to customers. We find some companies promising deliveries before the date the customer actually needs the product. When this situation occurs, the company is actually giving away delivery times (material and capacity) that could be used for other customers who may need the product sooner. Active management of the backlog and order promising function can assist in coping with the unpredictability of the timing for demand (see figures 7.5 and 7.6).

7. *Reschedule another customer's order.* When all avenues have been exhausted to meet a customer's requested delivery date, and material or capacity is unavailable because it's been promised to other customers, you still have one more alternative for meeting that customer's needs: promise the order and move another customer's order. This rescheduling alternative is often overlooked by sales and marketing people, who find the rescheduling process distasteful. Most company backlogs have customer orders scheduled to ship before the customer really needs the products, or there are orders in the backlog where the customers do not need the entire shipment. By managing the backlog and communicating with customers, customer delivery dates may be renegotiated so that all customers are satisfied with your company's performance.

When rescheduling to cope with the uncertainty of demand, the fol-

Figure 7.5
Master Production Schedule

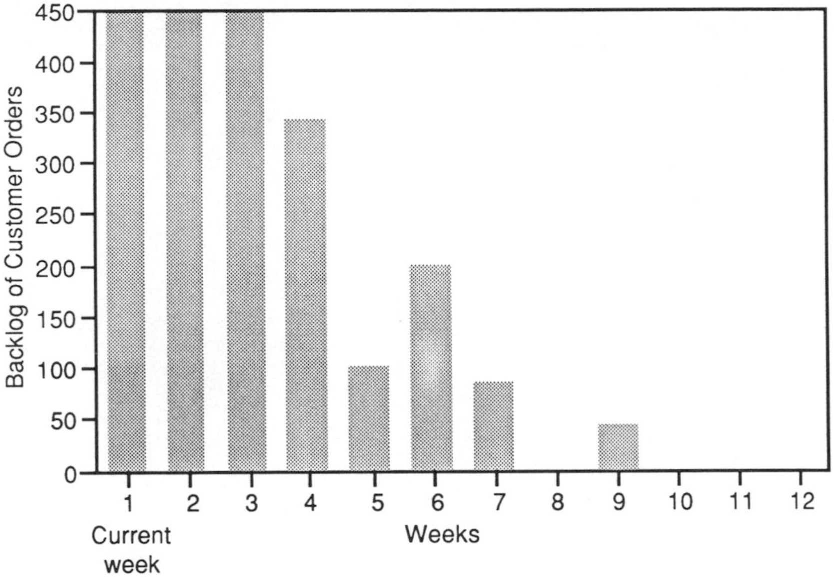

When customer orders are promised based upon the company's "best dates," the flexibility to deliver in near time frames is reduced as the schedule is fully loaded in near time frames.

lowing rule must be followed: entering an order with a fully committed Master Production Schedule requires that other orders be rescheduled out. If this rescheduling is not done, manufacturing quickly has an invalid Master Production Schedule and the company's priority system disintegrates. When there is more in the schedule than can be produced, manufacturing will be forced to select the orders it will build first, since numerous orders will all be late. Expediting starts to occur again, rendering the control system invalid.

Occasionally, it may be difficult to find a customer who is willing to accept a later delivery. When this situation occurs, it requires even more attention by the sales and marketing organization's customer service representatives. A vice president of a packaging equipment manufacturer in the Northwest refers to the process that occurs in this case as "pick a victim," since some customer is going to be dissatisfied.

Figure 7.6
Master Production Schedule

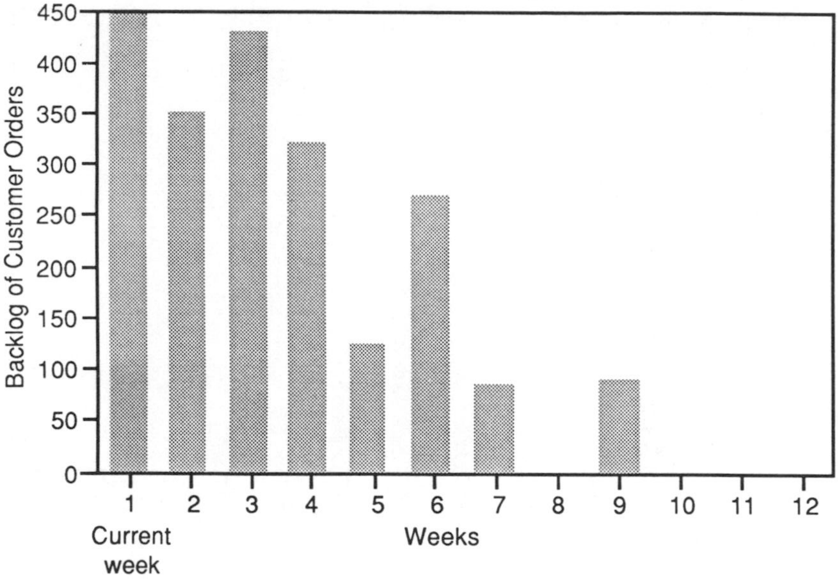

When customer orders are promised based upon customer "need dates," delivery flexibility is improved.

But the selection process has a positive side for sales and marketing: potentially, only one customer is unhappy. If the new order is simply crammed into the customer backlog without rescheduling, then many orders may ship late and many customers will be dissatisfied with the company's delivery performance. Most important, sales and marketing will be in control of who gets rescheduled.

We have found that Class A MRP II companies provide excellent customer service, even with the uncertainties of demand. These companies' customer service organizations realize that they play a key role in controlling customer satisfaction, but that the control comes not by "throwing orders over the wall" to manufacturing. It comes by assuming the responsibility for managing demand.

8. *Standardize products or options.* Often we find that companies have an opportunity to reduce the uncertainties in product mix or options through standardization. If the number of products or options can

be reduced without significant effect on demand, then forecast accuracy should improve. Not only is this situation statistically improved, but in addition, fewer items to forecast requires less time and resources.

An interesting and humorous book, *Clutter's Last Stand*, by Don Aslett, describes the costs and time associated with all the unused and unnecessary items we all have in our homes. Many of the concepts in the book apply directly to business as well as to personal situations, as many companies carry old, seldom-sold products or product options in their catalogs. This increases the company's database, which requires time and expense to maintain and keep current. Many companies are building a team with sales and marketing, engineering, and manufacturing to rid themselves of this "clutter" by continuously reviewing products for standardization and/or deproliferation of older or low volume items.

CUSTOMER SERVICE MEASUREMENTS AND FEEDBACK

To continuously improve, measurements and feedback are required. When you talk about measurements, however, people often become apprehensive. And rightfully so; for in many companies, measurements are used primarily to criticize individual performance rather than improve it. At one company, for instance, the forecaster's position was looked upon by other employees as certain death in career advancement within the company, because the company's management used forecast accuracy as the primary measurement of the forecaster's job performance. The forecasting accuracy levels were always below the company's stated standard, which had *never* been met. Two forecasters were terminated when the company did not achieve the business plan. Other forecasters simply quit or transferred to another position when they did not receive pay increases or advancement (see figure 7.7)

When the company embarked on a demand management program as part of its MRP II project, it was compelled to look beyond the forecaster in identifying the root cause of the forecasting inaccuracies. The experience caused the company to redefine its position on measure-

Figure 7.7

"Ms. Ryan, send me in a scapegoat."

From the Wall Street Journal—Permission, Cartoon Features Syndicate.

ments and to develop a measurements policy, which stated in part: "The purpose of measurements is to improve performance by identifying problem areas that are preventing the company from achieving greater success. The purpose of measurements is *not* to criticize individual performance. The expected response after measurements are made is to define problem areas, determine the cause(s) of the problems, identify solutions to the problems, and implement the recommended solutions."

It has often been said that "Anything measured gets better." We would change that to "Anything that is measured gets better—when the measurements are constructively applied to improving performance."

Three key measurements are generally made to determine the effectiveness of demand management efforts:

1. Customer service.
2. Performance to the sales plan.
3. Forecast accuracy.

CUSTOMER SERVICE MEASUREMENTS

The objective of your company's efforts in providing manufacturing quality, engineering design, sales coverage, etc. is to satisfy your customers' expectations. When you meet your customers' expectations, your company gains a marketing edge. Consequently, you should structure your measurements so they coincide with your customers' expectations. This requires that you determine what your customers view as important. Because customer expectations change, you must also periodically review and update your measurements to reflect changes in the marketplace. You also need to select measurements most suitable to your business situation. The following are two common types of customer service measurements:

1. *Line item fill rate.* This measurement is commonly employed in make-to-stock environments. Line item fill rate is a measurement (expressed in percentage) of how frequently product is available to ship from stock. For example, if a customer order includes ten line items, and the company is able to meet the customer's requirements on nine of those line items, the line item fill rate is 90 percent.

2. *Delivery as promised.* This measurement is typically used in a make-to-order situation. The shipment date is compared with the company's *original* promise date to determine what percentage of time the company ships its products to customers in accordance with the original promise. A tolerance may be established for the timing of the shipment (for example, ± 1 day), depending upon the particular customer's or marketplace's requirements. We have observed the tolerances becoming tighter and tighter over the past few years.

Tighter tolerances are being required by companies that are utilizing Just-in-Time manufacturing approaches. As part of their JIT efforts to eliminate waste, they are placing much more stringent requirements on their suppliers. A few years ago, suppliers were given some latitude in when they were required to deliver orders. It was not unusual for the delivery date to be stated, "During the week of . . ." Now, it is not unusual for a specific date to be specified, and some companies even require suppliers to deliver product in a specific hour, such as 10 a.m. on May 29th.

Another valuable measurement is the percentage of time that the promised delivery date meets the customer's requested delivery date. This measurement relates directly to the available-to-promise function in the Master Production Schedule and is a good indicator of how the company is meeting demand. If manufacturing is meeting its MPS objectives, but the percentage is decreasing, this usually indicates that demand is exceeding the original forecast. Conversely, if the percentage is constantly increasing, it may suggest that the forecast is too high.

The most important reason for making customer service measurements is to determine how customers are evaluating your performance. Consequently, don't fall into the trap of measuring yourself based upon your own biased beliefs. David Halberstam, in *The Reckoning*, relates how U.S. car manufacturers believed they were meeting customer expectations in the 1960s and early 1970s. Their measurements were based upon their own biases, however, and they did not truly reflect their customers' changing expectations. In contrast, Japanese car manufacturers were listening more intently to their customers and anticipated their changing expectations. Consequently, they were prepared to meet their customers' expectations, which eventually led to a major change in their share of the U.S. automobile market.

MEASUREMENT OF SALES PERFORMANCE TO PLAN

As we have discussed throughout the book, commitment to selling the plan is one of the keys to reducing the uncertainty of demand. By measuring how the sales force has performed in meeting demand, you can identify problem areas that are inhibiting the achievement of the plan. Performance to the plan should be measured by product family and should be reviewed at the monthly Sales and Operations Planning meeting. Feedback to the sales organization on how individual sales-people are perfoming to plan is key for continuous improvement.

When problem areas are identified, the TQC/Pareto approach described earlier can be utilized to determine the root cause of the problem. It is not uncommon to find that the root cause of the problem may not be a "sales" problem, but a problem in quality, pricing, or delivery. Or it may be indicative of an engineering or manufacturing problem. In one case we witnessed, the sales organization had received customer commitments to purchase a new product that the company was to introduce in the sixth month. Measurement of sales' perfor-mance to the plan in the sixth month indicated that bookings objectives had not been met. A detailed analysis revealed that bookings for one particular product—the new product—had not been achieved. The product had been delayed because it would not interface properly with automated test equipment. Again, the purpose of measurements is to identify and resolve problems.

FORECAST ACCURACY

Measurements of forecast accuracy at the detail level give you valu-able information on trends, product mix, and the uncertainty of de-mand. We are often asked how accurate the forecast must be to achieve Class A MRP II status. There is no one right answer to that question. What is more important than the accuracy of the forecast is the fore-casting process itself. Any measurement of forecasting accuracy should be used to determine the effectiveness of that process. In determining the effectiveness of the forecasting process, the following are some key questions that should be asked:

1. Does the forecasting process lead to a commitment to manufacture and sell to the plan?
2. Does it lead to an improved understanding of the customers and the marketplace?
3. Does it result in improved communications between all departments in the company that, in turn, enhances the performance of each de-partment?

In our opinion, answers to these questions should be affirmative, for these are the real measurements of forecasting performance.

We have seen some consultants' recommendations for establishing forecasting accuracy objectives of 95 percent in the aggregate and 85 percent in the mix or detail. While these are certainly good objectives, it is important to remember there are many variables for determining how the measurements are made, which in turn will affect the actual performance percentage. One of these variables is the timing of the measurements, specifically, when should the forecast be frozen for measurement purposes? Since the forecast is updated continuously, which forecast should be used as the reference for accuracy measurements?

We recommend that the forecast measurements be linked with the time fences for products. The forecast should be frozen for measurement purposes at each agreed-upon time fence; that is, save the forecast as it passes the time fence, then later compare actual demand with the original forecast. Since time fences represent points at which manufacturing's flexibility to respond to change is decreased, it is at these points that manufacturing has sufficient time to respond effectively to changes in the forecast. We do not recommend, however, that you freeze the forecast for communications purposes. If you know demand is changing inside a time fence, you have an obligation to communicate that situation to the company by changing the forecast. Your computer software should provide for the "freezing," or saving, of the forecast at time fences for measurement purposes, while allowing changes to be made inside the time fence (see figure 7.8).

THE MEANING OF MEASUREMENTS

A word of caution about interpreting demand management measurements: these measurements are a result of the total company's performance, and are not necessarily a measurement of an individual department's performance. It is, therefore, important that the company has a true understanding of how these measurements are affected by sales, marketing, manufacturing, engineering, and management. When

Figure 7.8

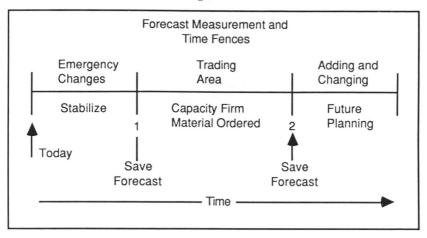

Forecasts at each time fence (1, 2) should be saved and compared with actual demand when making forecast accuracy measurements.

measuring the effectiveness of demand management, companies should consider other factors, including the following:

• Accuracy of assumptions, on which demand plans, sales plans, and forecasts are based.
• Lead times and backlogs.
• Inventory levels.

For measurements to help identify areas for improved performance, it is important that the results be communicated to the individuals responsible for meeting the plan in their specific area of accountability. Unfortunately, we find that many companies do not communicate the results of measurements unless there is a problem. It is just as important, perhaps more so, to let people know when the measurements show the company is being successful in achieving the plan. Good news is a stronger motivator than bad news. The communication of good news fosters commitment to continuously improve performance and helps unite all departments as a team to achieve the company's performance objectives.

PITFALLS AND TRAPS

Before we leave this chapter, it will be useful to review some of the danger areas that sales and marketing people are likely to encounter in the demand management process. You can increase the probability of success by avoiding the following pitfalls:

1. *Inaction.* Sales and marketing must take a leadership role if the company is to use manufacturing as a competitive weapon.
2. Failure of sales and marketing to understand the Master Production Schedule and available-to-promise function will lead to an inability to communicate with the rest of the company on issues of demand management.
3. Failure of sales and marketing to work with manufacturing to develop marketing/manufacturing strategies. As a result, the best marketing/manufacturing strategy may not be used to meet the delivery requirements of your customers.
4. If manufacturing is permitted to create too many items in the Master Production Schedule, your company may experience difficulty in both forecasting and communicating the forecast.
5. Failure to "consume" the forecast, resulting in frequent forecast changes being computed automatically by your software.
6. No recognition of abnormal demand in the order entry and Master Production Scheduling systems.
7. Relying too heavily on history for basing demand plans, sales plans, and forecasts.
8. Overlooking opportunities to link with customers.
9. Using measurements to criticize individual performance, rather than to identify problem areas for improving company performance.

CHECKLIST

1. Do you focus on improving forecasts by: (1) using qualified people for forecasting, (2) reviewing and updating the fore-

casts at least monthly, and (3) reconciling different views of the market?

2. Do you separate demands into streams and analyze each stream?

3. Do you manage each demand stream separately when appropriate?

4. Are all demand streams analyzed, including interplant, new-product, engineering, prototype, sample, and spare-parts demand?

5. Do you use Distribution Resource Planning to provide a communications link between warehouses or distribution centers and the demand planner, distribution management, and master scheduler?

6. Do you use TQC tools for analyzing and solving problems in reducing the uncertainty of demand?

7. Do you have well-thought-out strategies in place to cope with the uncertainty of demand?

8. Are measurements used to identify areas for improving company performance, rather than to criticize individual performance?

9. Do you base customer service measurements on your *customers'* expectations rather than on your own beliefs?

10. Do you measure the sales force's performance to plan and review the performance at the monthly Sales and Operations Planning meeting? Is feedback provided?

11. Do you strive to avoid common pitfalls that can hinder the success of demand management efforts?

Chapter 8

Steps for Getting Started in Gaining a Marketing Edge

It is the spirit of the men who follow and of the man who leads that gains the victory.

—George S. Patton

The purpose of this book has been to describe how demand management unites sales and marketing and manufacturing in a cooperative effort to gain a marketing advantage. That sales and marketing take a leadership role in managing demand is imperative to successfully gain a marketing edge. This book will only be of value, however, if you take the insights we have presented and put them to work.

Too often, we find that companies establish programs, like MRP II/JIT/TQC, and then believe their work is done. But the purpose of these programs is to continually produce high quality products at low costs and to make those products available when the customer needs them. This is an ongoing challenge, and the work is never done.

So where do you begin? If you are fortunate enough to already have MRP II or JIT/TQC in place, you are already a large step ahead of the game. A level of understanding already exists within your company that will foster a ready acceptance of and commitment to demand management.

If your company has not yet employed MRP II, then you have a greater—but not impossible—task ahead. First, you will have to convince your own company of the benefits of using its manufacturing resource as a competitive weapon. And this may take time to accomplish, because it usually requires a major philosophical change from traditional manufacturing management practices.

In either case, the steps for implementation are the same:

1. Gain understanding through education. Change is difficult for everyone. When people understand why change is needed, it is adopted more readily, and people become committed to new ways of doing business. By educating the management team on the fundamentals of MRP II/JIT/TQC, they will understand how to achieve the company's competitive objectives. Teamwork is often started by education in outside classes with management attending the classes together. In this way, they start building the company team with a mutual level of understanding.

2. Provide leadership through example and provide guidance and direction. Don't wait for another department to take the reins. As Bob Donath, editor of *Business Marketing* magazine, so aptly observed in a March 1985 article, "Marketers who ignore their leadership role intrinsic to MRP simply won't survive. The rest will either love MRP or hate it, but either way, they'll be in the driver's seat with no place to hide."

3. Dedicate resources to the demand planning/management function. For a program to be successful, someone must coordinate the efforts of the sales and marketing organization through implementation and on an ongoing basis.

4. Review your marketing/manufacturing strategy. Now is the time to reassess how you define "where you meet the customer."

5. Start the Sales and Operations Planning process. If you already conduct monthly staff meetings, turn them into forward-looking sessions that result in time phased sales and manufacturing plans.

6. Develop an effort to improve the forecast, and strive to turn forecasts into committed sales plans with responsibility and accountability clearly defined.

7. Manage demand as forecasts turn into actual orders. Step up to the responsibility of ensuring that your company meets its customers' expectations. Do not abdicate the responsibility to others in the company.

8. Establish measurements and controls on the demand management

process. Use them to increase your understanding of your company's performance in satisfying its customers' needs and to identify further improvements needed to achieve a marketing advantage.

9. Understand that MRP II/JIT/TQC are continuous processes. Once begun, they have no end; meeting your customers' expectations is an ever-changing and never-ending process.

Finally, as you attend to the details, large and small, don't lose sight of the overall purpose of your efforts: to form a cooperative team to better utilize your company's resources. When this objective is achieved, the quality of life for sales and marketing as well as manufacturing improves dramatically. Manufacturing people can concentrate their efforts on improving product quality and production efficiency, rather than coping with the crisis of past-due orders. The sales force can spend its time dealing with customers and developing new business rather than fighting with the factory to expedite deliveries.

And most important of all, when a company delivers a quality product at a reasonable price, on time as promised, it gains satisfied, long-term customers. This is what the marketing edge is all about.

Appendix A

Turnaround Tools: MRP II/JIT/TQC

Throughout the book, we have discussed Manufacturing Resource Planning, Just-in-Time, and Total Quality Control. Following is a brief synopsis of these programs and how companies are using these programs as tools to become more competitive, productive, and profitable.

MANUFACTURING RESOURCE PLANNING (MRP II)

Manufacturing Resource Planning is a proven methodology for managing a manufacturing business. While MRP II has been defined in many ways, one of the best descriptions is offered by Tom Wallace in his book, *MRP II: Making it Happen.* According to Wallace, MRP II embodies

. . . a method for the effective planning of all resources of a manufacturing company. Ideally, it addresses operational planning in units, financial planning in dollars, and has a simulation capability to answer "what if" questions. It is made up of a variety of functions, each linked together: business planning, sales and operations planning, master production scheduling, material requirements planning, capacity requirements planning and the execution support systems for capacity and material. Output from these systems would be integrated with financial reports such as the business plan, purchase commitment reports, shipping budget, inventory projections in dollars, etc. Manufacturing Resource Planning is a direct outgrowth and expression of closed loop MRP. MRP II has also been defined, validly, as a management system based on network scheduling. Also, and perhaps best, as *organized common sense*.

Properly implemented, MRP II is a powerful means of controlling the business. It is used by everyone from the CEO to the shop floor supervisor, thereby encompassing all organizations of the company—manufacturing, sales and marketing, finance, engineering, quality assurance, and all support functions.

Manufacturing Resource Planning evolved from "Material Requirements Planning" (MRP), which began in the 1960s when modern computing power became available to manufacturing companies. Initially, MRP was used as a way to order materials, and later to schedule them. MRP would take product bills of materials and "explode" them into "time phased" arrays based on requirement dates and lead times that would assist the production and inventory control department in material planning. This represented a major improvement over previously used techniques of inventory management, such as "order point," which failed to adequately plan for necessary components during periods of change, since it determines when to order by historical usage only.

As MRP became more popular and proved itself, companies began using it to plan for capacity as well as materials. This also paved the way for the use of MRP in a variety of different industries. Initially, it was used primarily by manufacturing companies in an assembled product environment. In the early 1970s, MRP found its way into process industries, such as pharmaceuticals, textiles, and chemicals.

It soon became apparent that MRP was a powerful management tool, and by the mid 1970s people spoke of the "closed loop" concept in which MRP was seen as a manufacturing control system. More benefits of MRP were eventually discovered in the 1970s, such as its use in vendor scheduling, which tied suppliers more directly to a manufacturer.

In the late 1970s and early 1980s, MRP became used as a system for customer order scheduling and financial management of the company. It was at this time, in 1979, because of the significant changes that had taken place in MRP methodology, that Oliver Wight, in conjunction with *Modern Materials Handling* magazine, coined the phrase "Manufacturing Resource Planning (MRP II)." Wight wanted to distinguish Manufacturing Resource Planning (MRP II) from Material Requirements Planning (MRP) in that the former implied a total system of running a company, while the latter was only concerned with ordering materials and scheduling the work flow on the factory floor. MRP II had, in fact, evolved into a simple systematic process for translating high level plans into specific day-to-day tasks (see figure A-1).

Today, it is widely recognized that MRP II is essential to the success of a manufacturing company, regardless of its industry. This is evidenced by looking at the results of an exhaustive survey conducted by the Oliver Wight Companies in 1985: 98 percent of the Class A MRP II users gained improvement in "better control of the business" and 96 percent had increases in customer service. Eighty percent of the Class A companies indicated their performance was "enormously better" than before implementation of MRP II. Our own personal experiences in manufacturing companies before implementation of MRP II and after reaching Class A status are what prompted the writing of this book. The difference is like night and day.

Doesn't MRP II mean a large investment in hardware and software, though? Possibly, depending on your company's current data processing capabilities. More important, implementing MRP II means investing in the education and training of your personnel. It is now recognized that although software is essential to succeeding with MRP II, the people factor is even more important. You can take the most functionally complete piece of MRP II software and put it in the hands of unqualified people, only to achieve poor results. Conversely, you can take an MRP II package with minimal functionality and achieve superior results if the people in the company are properly trained and motivated. The key point is that while a functional data processing

Figure A.1

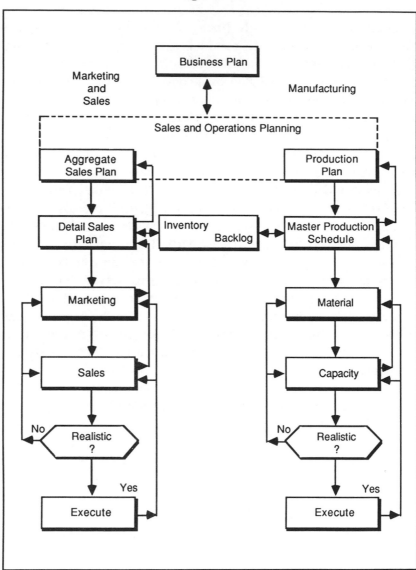

The closed loop MRP II process.

system is essential, people make things happen. MRP II is *not* a manufacturing software package; it is a different way of managing the business.

JUST-IN-TIME/TOTAL QUALITY CONTROL

Every company strives to reduce costs, inventories, and lead times while simultaneously trying to improve quality and customer service. JIT is a philosophy and organized methodology for continuously striving to meet those objectives. We particularly like the definition and approach taken by Bill Sandras, of Productivity Centers International of Johnstown, Colorado, and an Oliver Wight Education Associate. He describes JIT as a "philosophy with a methodology to *continuously and relentlessly* eliminate waste." Waste is defined as "any non-value added effort."

Credit is generally given to the Japanese, specifically at Toyota Motor Corporation, for developing Just-in-Time as a modern manufacturing practice. Taiiche Ohno of Toyota once described Just-in-Time as "a pillar of the production system" for building cars at his company. Ohno defined waste as "anything other than the minimum amount for the materials, manpower, machines or tools necessary for production." When JIT was first introduced in the United States, it was understood to be a means for reducing inventory. Now there is a growing awareness that the reduction in inventory that occurs with JIT is a natural consequence of the process of eliminating waste throughout the entire company.

JIT offers major benefits to manufacturers in terms of improved quality, lower costs, and reduced physical space required to build the product. Companies that have actively pursued a JIT philosophy have achieved amazing results in shortening their manufacturing build time and increasing flexibility, thereby gaining the ability to be more responsive to changes in demand. While MRP II provides a means for *controlling* the manufacturing environment, JIT is a means for *stimulating changes* (improvements) in the environment. At one Hewlett-Packard division, for example, work-in-process inventory dollars dropped 82 percent after the implementation of JIT. At the same division, floor space was reduced 40 percent, scrap and rework were reduced 30 percent, product build time was reduced 85 percent, labor efficiency increased 50 percent, and shipments increased by 20 percent. Conservative estimates of typical results of JIT include: 50 percent reduction in throughput time, 50 percent reduction in scrap and rework, 50 to 90 percent reduction in setup times, 40 to 50 percent reduction in required manufacturing space, and 10 to 100 percent improvement in quality specifics. Most companies that implement JIT achieve a fivefold improvement in overall quality and tenfold improvement in inventory turns in three to seven years.

The underlying rationale for JIT is to improve continuously the ability to respond to changes in the marketplace with a minimum amount of waste. Companies obviously must change to respond to fluctuations in the marketplace. But the costs of such changes are often staggering. Excess and unnecessary facilities, machinery, and manufacturing capacity represent one kind of cost. Unnecessary administrative personnel and excessive and obsolete inventory are examples of other costs.

One of the practices of a JIT philosophy is that a company carry no more inventory than is necessary to meet demand. This means that the quality of all materials and components must be as close to perfect as possible, since any products that need to be scrapped or returned will cause a shortage. This practice is a driving force for Total Quality Control, not only for your factory, but for your vendors.

JIT exposes problems, such as shortages, while Total Quality Control is used to eliminate those problems. The key point we wish to make, however, is that the truly successful manufacturers are not those that have picked one ''solution'' to their problem, but have learned to *integrate* their efforts. JIT, TQC, and MRP II all go hand in hand. Top performance is achieved by those companies that do all three simultaneously—in concert.

We wish to point out that MRP II, JIT, and TQC are not the answer to being competitive. Rather, the answer lies in simultaneous improvements in performance—quality, delivery, cost, and service. MRP II, JIT, and TQC are simply tools for helping your company become more competitive, productive, and profitable.

Since quality is improved under the JIT philosophy, rework and scrap is minimized, which improves costs. Also, because JIT brings in only what you need, as you need it, your warehouse and factory space can be smaller. This in turn leads to reduced handling costs. Overall, your cost of creating product will drop, which will allow you to adopt more competitive pricing policies.

In addition to better quality and pricing, JIT can allow you to offer better customer service. Since JIT strives to eliminate wasted time, manufacturing lead times will be reduced constantly, resulting in shorter customer lead times and more timely response to stock outs. And the shorter the time to make a product, the more responsive your company will be to actual customer demand, thereby improving the company's overall performance.

JIT allows a company to respond more quickly to changes in market demand. Shorter cumulative manufacturing lead times provide for more manufacturing responsiveness. As we discussed earlier, the company that can respond quickly to change has the best chances of getting and staying ahead over the long haul.

A tremendous amount has been written about quality during the past few years. Many companies are achieving great results in improved company performance through their quality programs. The work of W. Edwards Deming, J. M. Juran, and Phil Crosby has stimulated a significant sector of American industry to concentrate on quality and to use it to improve their overall company performance. The Tennant Company, a Class A MRP II firm, has had such success with its quality program that the company published a book, *Quest for Quality*, in which its program and successes are discussed.

Looking In

When your company implements Just-in-Time, marketing and sales will receive a number of benefits, including higher quality, shorter customer lead times, and lower costs. It doesn't take most marketing and sales people long to use these benefits to their competitive advantage.

As with most things in business, however, benefits do not come free, and marketing and sales must contribute to the Just-in-Time effort. As the wasteful activities of the company come under scrutiny through the JIT/TQC process, the traditions of the company will be, and should be, changed. The number and configurations of products will be questioned. The need for thousands of products or options (often never sold) and the requirement to provide another "1967 version" of the product will come under attack. Your business may require long-term support of products, but selling outdated products to new customers will be questioned. The entire company must rethink the way it has done things historically and how it is currently doing things; marketing and sales functions are part of the reformulation. Walt Goddard, in his book *Just-in-Time, Surviving by Breaking Tradition*, said it well when he wrote, "So much of the implementation of Just-in-Time depends on people willing to change. Marketing is no exception." The good news is that as the changes occur, the customer ultimately benefits, and when the customer benefits, marketing and the entire company benefits.

LOOKING OUT

Once your company has its manufacturing under control and is constantly improving through its MRP II/JIT/TQC efforts, the marketing and sales organizations can use the enhanced company performance as a selling tool. A manufacturer in the Midwest recently told us how its salespeople carry charts of customer service with them showing on-time delivery performance (consistently 98 percent or better). When confronted with a competitive situation or a customer negotiation, the salespeople use the chart to reinforce their arguments and overcome customer objections. Tellabs, a manufacturer of high-speed telecommunications equipment and a Class A MRP II/JIT/TQC organization, uses its manufacturing department as a sales tool. Ed McDevitt, vice president of manufacturing, spends as much as one day per week on the road marketing Just-in-Time to customers. Perhaps the best benefit of all is that once a company has established a reputation for consistent on-time, high-quality delivered products, the competition must work especially hard to cut into the business.

A significant change has occurred in many industries in the 1980s due to a number of economic factors. More and more companies are

Figure A.2

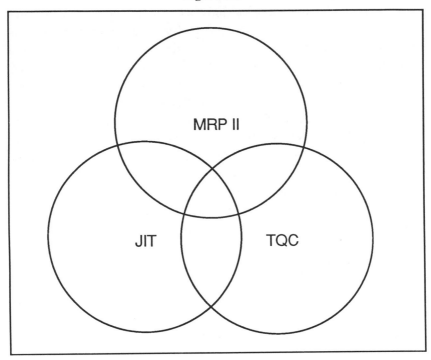

The efforts of MRP II/JIT/TQC complement each other to improve your competitive position.

now basing purchasing decisions on an analysis of total cost/total value rather than just price. And when your company consistently ships quality product on time as promised, this adds both to the perceived and real value to the purchaser.

MRP II/JIT/TQC has implications for sales and marketing when selling to customers who have implemented similar manufacturing philosophies and techniques. The expectations of these customers become higher with regards to vendor performance, and the requirements to keep their business become more demanding. Many manufacturers are now reducing their total number of vendors based upon the vendors' performance in the areas of quality, delivery, service, and price. The old tradition of getting multiple bids and taking the lowest price is being replaced by new, closer relationships between a company and its suppliers. Xerox, for example, has reduced its total number of vendors from over five thousand to less than three hundred. As a sales and marketing professional, one would hope to be one of the three hundred.

During a conversation with a gasket manufacturer who services a major automotive manufacturer, we learned that the automotive manufacturer reduced its number of approved vendors for one line of gaskets from *140 to 2!* We had this conversation with the gasket maker at an MRP II class for sales and marketing personnel. He indicated the reason he was there was to make sure he *remained* one of the two or became the *one* approved vendor.

The standards of manufacturers as they measure vendor performance are also becoming more and more stringent. It is typical to find on-time delivery now being defined, for example, as $+0, -2$ days, at *his* dock. This means the manufacturer is allowing no late deliveries and will not accept deliveries of products more than two days early at his facility. Some manufacturers are even operating under a synchronized scheduling system with their vendors in which delivery must be made within specific *hourly* time frames. Quality measurements have become even more demanding, with manufacturers expecting to receive zero defect, or 100 percent quality products.

What this means to sales and marketing organizations of companies supplying these manufacturers is that the rules have changed. If your company hasn't changed its operating philosophy, methodologies, and systems, chances are these customers will be unavailable to you in the future. But if your company is one of the few that elects to be a world-class performer, then these customers offer a tremendous opportunity as other suppliers fail to meet the requirements imposed by them.

Another benefit of selling to customers who are operating with MRP II/JIT/TQC is the opportunity to reduce the uncertainty of demand (reduce forecast error) through a process of customer linking. This process takes your customer's plans (vendor schedules) and shares them with you on a regular basis. You therefore know to the best of their knowledge what it is they plan to purchase from you. When manufacturing and sales and marketing have access to this type of customer information, a better understanding of future demands is achieved.

One of the side benefits of customer linking is the building of strong relationships with your customers. When you are sharing detailed plans with one another, the bond between you becomes stronger, making it more difficult for competition to penetrate your special accounts.

Sources for Additional Information

Preparing yourself to implement a Class A MRP II system requires careful study of a huge amount of information, far more than could be included in this or any other book. The Oliver Wight Companies can provide further assistance in getting ready, including books on the subject, live education, and reviews of commercially available software packages.

OLIVER WIGHT EDUCATION ASSOCIATES

OWEA is made up of a group of independent MRP II educators and consultants around the world who share a common philosophy and common goals. Classes directed toward both upper- and middle-level management are being taught in various locations around the U.S. and Canada, as well as abroad. For a detailed class brochure, listing course descriptions, instructors, costs, dates, and locations, or for the name of a recommended consultant in your area, please contact:

Oliver Wight Education Associates
P.O. Box 435
Newbury, NH 03255
800-258-3862 or 603-763-5926

OLIVER WIGHT VIDEO PRODUCTIONS, INC.

The Oliver Wight Video Library offers companies the video-based materials they need to teach the "critical mass" of their employees about the principles of MRP II and Just-in-Time. For more information on obtaining the Oliver Wight Video Library, contact:

Oliver Wight Video Productions, Inc.
5 Oliver Wight Drive
Essex Junction, VT 05452
800-343-0625 or 802-878-8161

Index